A~Z

OF

SEWING

FOR SMOCKERS

INSPIRATIONS BOOKS

Have you ever been frustrated by sleeves that won't sit properly or a hemline that droops? What is the difference between a sleeve cuff and a sleeve band? Does the stitching show on your piping no matter how hard you try to avoid it? How do you trim a collar so that it has a perfectly curved edge? The answers to all of these questions, plus many more, are contained within the pages of this book, the perfect companion to the A-Z of Smocking.

Over the years we have received countless requests from our readers to produce a manual of construction techniques for smocked garments. Many of these requests have come from enthusiastic stitchers who love to sit and smock but are daunted when it comes to putting a garment together. In this book we de-mystify the process through clear step-by-step photographs and concise instructions designed to guide you effortlessly from start to finish.

Many of the techniques covered in this book have a long history, some are newer approaches to old problems. Scattered throughout the pages you will find helpful hints and tips to make your task even easier.

All are tried and tested methods that will help you to produce beautifully constructed and finished garments.

HAPPY STITCHING,

Susan O'Connor

SUSAN O'CONNOR

CONTENTS

EQUIPMENT

Like most tasks, constructing a smocked garment is made easier
if you have the right equipment.

SEWING MACHINES

A sewing machine is a vital piece of equipment for quick construction of a garment. A machine is a major investment and can cost as little as a few hundred or as much as many thousands of dollars. Look carefully at what is available and choose a machine that best suits your needs. Constructing a smocked garment requires very basic machine features such as straight and zigzag stitches and a good buttonhole. It is a waste to spend dollars on extra features that you will never use.

Position the machine on a flat, even working surface with adequate surrounding space to store other sewing requirements.

Once you have a machine, taking good care of it ensures that it will last a long time.

Fluff and dust will collect under the base plate and should be removed regularly to keep the machine running smoothly.

This is particularly important if sewing velvet, corduroy or any other pile fabric that will shed large amounts of fibre.

Regular oiling will keep the machine running smoothly. Read the machine manual to determine if, where and how often the machine should be oiled. Have it serviced annually by a qualified mechanic and keep it covered and in a dry place when not in use.

If travelling with your machine, place a piece of soft fabric on the base plate and ensure that the presser foot is down. Computerised machines can be temperamental and may not like being moved at all.

MACHINE PRESSER FEET

Sewing machines come with several interchangeable feet, each one designed for a specific purpose. Read the machine manual to determine the correct use for each foot. It is well worth purchasing a twin needle foot if your machine does not come with one.

SCISSORS

Good quality, sharp dressmaking scissors will make cutting out the garment easy.

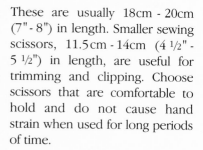

These are usually 18cm - 20cm (7" - 8") in length. Smaller sewing scissors, 11.5cm - 14cm (4 ½" - 5 ½") in length, are useful for trimming and clipping. Choose scissors that are comfortable to hold and do not cause hand strain when used for long periods of time.

Scissors are available with metal, plastic or special 'soft grip' handles. If you suffer from arthritis, you may find scissors with larger finger holes helpful. Use the full blade when cutting as this ensures a straight cut edge.

Have scissors professionally sharpened as soon as they show signs of wear. Dead spots along the length or at the tip of the scissor blades are a common sign of wear. Take extra care not to drop scissors as this can damage the blades beyond repair.

Keep scissors lubricated by occasionally placing a small drop of oil onto the screw. Wipe away any excess before using.

Store scissors in a safe place to ensure that they are not used inappropriately.

THREAD NIPPERS

These handy thread clips are useful for general trimming and getting into tight spots. They can be hung around the neck or kept close to the sewing machine.

ROTARY CUTTERS

Excellent for cutting bias or straight strips of fabric and other cutting jobs. Replace the blade as soon as it shows wear. Usually used in conjunction with a special cutting mat.

CUTTING TABLES

If you have space, a cutting table gives a wonderful surface for laying and cutting out fabric.

Most cutting tables are light-weight and can be folded up and stored away.

SEAM RIPPERS

A good seam ripper or quick unpick is invaluable when sewing. This handy little tool makes unpicking easy by cutting the sewing threads along the seam. It is also used to cut open machine buttonholes after they are stitched. Keep one handy by your sewing machine.

FABRIC MARKERS

Marking pens are very handy for transferring any temporary pattern or design markings onto fabric. There are several different types available so choose the one that best suits your needs.

Water-soluble markers

These are chemical based and leave blue marks that can be removed with water. Do not iron before removing as heat may affect the marks and make them difficult to remove.

Fade-away markers

These are also chemical based, leave a purple mark and will fade away by themselves. This can happen in five minutes or take several hours. Do not iron before removing.

Chalk-based pencils

These are excellent for use on dark coloured fabrics as they come in white, pink and blue. The chalk 'lead' is enclosed in wood, making them easy to use. Sharpen regularly as the soft chalk blunts easily.

Tailor's chalk

This comes in a pressed block, and is the forerunner of the pencil. Both chalk based products are removed by brushing or sponging with a damp cloth.

RULERS AND TAPE MEASURES

Long rulers (metal or wood)

Useful for marking long lines on fabric such as cutting lines, bindings and bias strips.

Dressmaker's squares

Useful for checking if fabric is true to grain and determining the true bias. They are invaluable for ruling lines that are at right angles to each other.

Tape measures

A tape measure is a pliable measuring device useful for all types of measuring jobs. Choose a tape that begins the numbering from both ends and has metric and imperial measurements.

NEEDLES

Sewing machine needles are available in different sizes, ranging from the finest (size 60) to the coarsest (size 110). Choose a needle that is suited to the type and weight of fabric that you are using and replace it regularly. Discard needles that are bent or burred as they can cause irreparable damage to fabric and are difficult to stitch with. A damaged needle can also result in the machine skipping stitches. Hand sewing needles are essential for all of those small stitching jobs that cannot be done on the machine. A crewel (embroidery) needle is suitable for most tasks such as tacking, slipstitching, hemming, sewing on buttons, working thread loops and sewing on trims.

Type	Description	Use	Suitable for	Size
Universal	Standard	Standard clothing	Almost every natural and synthetic fabric chiffon, georgette, organdy, batiste	60, 70
			Artificial silk, linen blends, lingerie fabrics poplin, shirting	70, 80
			Ticking, linen, suiting	80, 90
			Coating	90, 100
Jersey/Stretch	Ball Point	Knit garments Swimwear	Fine jersey, single jersey	70
			Jersey, silk jersey	75
			Lycra, lingerie fabrics	80, 90
			Knits (interlock, rugby)	90, 100
Jeans	Extra sharp	Outer garments Sportswear	Canvas, cord, denim, heavy twill	90 - 110
Microtex	Extra sharp	Standard clothing	Microfibre, silk	60 - 80
Embroidery	Large eye, highly polished hollow neck, light ball point	Embroidery and specialty threads	Any natural or synthetic fabrics	75 - 90
Hemstitch	Wing needle	Embroidery, hemstitching	Various natural fibre fabrics	100
Quilting	Light point	Straight and top stitching, decorative stitching	Any natural or synthetic fabrics	75 - 90
Twin Needle	Standard needle double shaft	Tucks, embroidery	Light to medium weight natural or synthetic fabric	70 - 100
Triple Needle	Standard needle triple shaft	Tucks, embroidery	Light to medium weight natural or synthetic fabric	80

PINS

A wide variety of pins is available, varying in length, diameter and type of head. It is well worth investing in several packets of fine, glass headed pins that will last for many years and make pinning a pleasure. Glass heads will not melt if ironed and are easy to find if dropped onto the floor. Silk pins have longer and finer shafts than regular pins and glide easily through most fabrics. They are available with plain or glass heads. Discard any pins that are burred, bent or damaged in any way. Store pins in a sealed, moisture-proof container to prevent rust.

Description	Head	Diameter	Length	Use	Metal
Dressmaker	Metal	0.85mm	48mm	Heavy fabric	Hardened steel
Dressmaker	Metal	0.70mm	32mm	Light fabric	Hardened steel
Dressmaker	Metal	0.65mm	25mm	Light and medium fabric	Hardened steel
Dressmaker	Metal	0.60mm	30mm	Light and medium fabric	Hardened steel
Dressmaker	Metal	0.50mm	30mm	Delicate fabric	Hardened steel
Couture	Metal	0.58mm	25mm	Light and medium fabric	Stainless steel
Dressmaker	Metal	0.65mm	27mm	Light and medium fabric	Nickel plated steel
Dressmaker	Metal	0.70mm	32mm	Light and medium fabric	Nickel plated steel
Lace	Metal	0.65mm	25mm	Lace	Brass
Glass head	Glass	0.60mm	30mm	Light and medium fabric	Nickel plated steel
Glass head	Glass	0.50mm	35mm	Light and delicate fabric	Nickel plated steel
Flower head	Plastic	0.55mm	50mm	Light and delicate fabric	Nickel plated steel
Patchwork (extra sharp)	Glass	0.50mm	36mm	Light and medium fabric	Nickel plated steel

THIMBLES

Thimbles are available in a number of different materials including plastic, leather, metal and ceramic. A thimble protects the top of the finger that is used to push the needle through the fabric. Choose a thimble that fits snugly over your finger.

IRONS

Irons can vary from simple models that cost a few dollars, to deluxe ironing systems that include large water reservoirs and suction boards. Common problems with irons are scale buildup in the water tank and a dirty soleplate. Using distilled water or buying an iron with a filter can help to alleviate the scale problem. Cleaning the iron regularly will keep the soleplate in good order.

PUFF IRONS

An ingenious device for pressing puffed sleeves. The egg shaped tool is clamped to a table top. The sleeve is rubbed over the heated puff iron to remove any creases.

IRONING BOARDS

Choose a sturdy board with a smooth padded cover. Keep the cover clean to prevent dirt transferring to the fabric that is being pressed.

SLEEVE BOARDS

A sleeve board is a smaller version of an ironing board. It enables you to press a greater variety of garments and their component parts in the round.

PRESSING HAMS

A pressing ham takes its name from its similarity in shape to the cured meat. It is a very firmly filled pillow of fabric, usually wool on one side and cotton on the other. A ham is used for pressing small areas that are difficult to reach on a flat surface. It is also used for pressing curves and rolling collars.

PRESSING ROLLS

A sleeve roll is similar to a ham but cylindrical in shape. It is particularly useful for pressing sleeves and other parts of a garment that cannot be laid flat.

PRESSING MITTS

A glove shaped pressing device, the mit is worn on the hand and pushed into areas that cannot be laid flat.

PRESSING CLOTHS

Chemically treated pressing cloths are known as rajah cloths. They are used when steam ironing and are excellent for setting pleats and removing creases. Rectangles of cotton fabric are useful for pressing delicate fabrics, fusing interfacing and appliqué.

Flannelette or fine towelling are helpful when pressing embroidery. Fold the fabric into a pad, place beneath the embroidery and press the back of the fabric.

VELVET BOARDS OR PIN BOARDS

A pin board is invaluable when using fabric with a nap such as corduroy or velvet. It resembles a miniature bed of nails. The fabric is laid face down onto the board and pressed from the back. The pins prevent the nap from being pressed flat.

FABRICS

Fabric is the foundation for every garment and there is an enormous range available for making into smocked clothing. They can be made of natural fibres, synthetic fibres or a combination of the two. Natural fibres such as pure cotton, linen and silk crease easily so they should be chosen for garments that will not be spoiled by wrinkling. Manmade fibres such as polyester are added to natural fibres to help eliminate crushability. Your choice of fabric will be determined by several factors including budget, availability and function of the garment. When buying fabric, take note of the care requirements and pre-wash fabrics that may shrink.

Always test pleat a sample of the fabric you intend to use to determine its suitability before beginning a project. When test pleating, use the same number of needles that you will use in the actual project. A fabric that pleats easily with only a few needles may behave differently with twenty-four needles. Use a 30cm (12") width of fabric as a sample piece.

Check the entire length of fabric for faults or flaws before positioning the pattern and cutting out. Remove selvedges.

Ensure that the cut ends of the fabric are straight and follow the grainline. This can be done by pulling a thread across the width and cutting along this line. Most fabrics will tear along the weft grainline but care must be taken that this does not stretch the torn edge or create bruising in the fabric. Once the ends are straightened, check that the fabric is running true to the grain. The warp and weft threads should be resting at right angles to one another. If they are not the straight edge of the fabric will not be at a right angle to the

selvedge. Re-align the threads by pulling the fabric at the diagonal corners.

Before pleating printed fabrics, check that the print runs true to the weft grainline. If not, once the fabric is pleated, the print can create unsightly sloping lines.

Most fabrics will have the print running true to the selvedge. In some cases, it is preferable to pleat the fabric down the selvedge. It will then be necessary to cut all pattern pieces this way.

In some instances the best solution can be to pleat the fabric following the print rather than the grain. It is often useful to pleat using half space rows as the pleats are more likely to bubble and twist.

TERMINOLOGY

Selvedge

The reinforced edge of the fabric. It can be closely woven so trim it away before pleating and constructing the garment.

Warp and weft threads

The names for the two sets of threads that are required for the manufacture of woven fabrics.

Warp threads are the weaving threads that run from the front to the back of the weaving loom, parallel to the selvedge.

Weft threads, or filling, are the set of weaving threads that run across the warp threads from selvedge to selvedge.

Grain

The direction of the warp or weft of the fabric.

Bias

An oblique direction to the warp and the weft. The true bias is at an angle of 45° from both the warp and weft. A bias cut is also known as cutting on the cross.

Plump, round pleats are a pleasure to smock on but not all fabrics have sufficient body to give a satisfactory result. Round pleats occupy more space, therefore less fabric is required to provide a good working surface.

There are two easy ways to add body to fabric -

1. Starch and press the area that is to be pleated with a good quality starch. Several light sprays are preferable to one soaking spray.

2. Fuse lightweight interfacing across the back of the area to be pleated.

Unwashed fabric contains sizing or finishing that increases the body of the fabric. Avoid pre-washing unless it is necessary as the sizing will hold the pleats nicely.

Pre-wash interfacing if recommended by the manufacturer.

Layering fabric will also provide a good working surface as you will be stitching through a double thickness. Choose fabrics that can be laundered in the same way.

HINT

Always pleat fabric before selecting your threads. Pleated fabric can look quite different to unpleated fabric.

TYPES OF FABRIC

The following fabrics are the most commonly used for smocking.

Batiste

The First Step, AS&E 41

Soft, fine, lightweight fabric named after the French weaver, Jean Batiste. It has a slightly heavier fibre gauge and density than voile, but is still a translucent fabric suitable for similar appli-cations to voile. Easy to pleat, it may be made of cotton, linen, silk, synthetic or blended fibres. Cotton or cotton blends can be handwashed. Silk batiste should be drycleaned.

Broadcloth

Fine, tightly woven fabric with a faint rib. Originally made of mercerised cotton, it is now made of any fibre. It is easy to pleat and care advice corresponds to the type of fibre - cotton and cotton blends can be gentle machine washed, silk should be drycleaned.

Challis

A soft, lightweight, plain weave fabric, originally made from wool but now also manufactured from synthetic fibres. It is often printed in small floral or paisley designs and is suitable for winter garments. Wool challis feeds through the pleater with relative ease, but the pleats 'pop' out readily. When pleating, use half space rows and pack and steam the pleats to help them hold their shape. Using a dense smocking design is recommended for the same reason. Wool challis should be drycleaned to minimize shrinkage. Synthetic challis fabrics should be laundered according to the manufacturer's instructions.

Chambray

Eliza, AS&E 37

A cotton, silk or cotton blend, plain weave fabric where the warp threads are coloured (blue is common) and the weft threads are white. It may incorporate checks, stripes or small figured or dobby patterns and is generally a medium weight fabric used for garments. Most chambray fabrics should pleat easily. Cotton and cotton blends can be machine washed.

Corduroy

Precious Coral, AS&E 44

A corded fabric where the weft pile forms ribs, also known as wales, that have been sheared or woven to produce a smooth, velvet-like nap.

The wales vary in width from jumbo to the very fine featherwale. Traditionally made of cotton, it is made of many different fibres today. Featherwale, also known as 21 wale, or baby wale is the most suitable corduroy for smocking and is easy to pleat. Slightly heavier weight corduroys may be used but test pleating is strongly recommended, otherwise bent and broken pleater needles may result.

Prevent excessive fraying by overlocking or machine neatening cut edges. As this fabric has a nap, follow pattern layouts according to the 'with nap' instructions. Generally hand or machine wash in warm water, and iron on the wrong side of the fabric to avoid crushing the pile.

Crêpe

Gifts from the Sea, AS&E 47

A term used to describe all types of fabrics regardless of fibre composition that have a crinkly, crimped or grained surface. The pleatability and care instructions will vary depending on the fibres used, density of the weave and stiffness of the fabric. Test pleat before beginning a project and follow the manufacturer's care instructions.

Damask

Fabric woven on a Jacquard loom to produce satin weave in areas of pattern against a plain or twill background so that light will be reflected from the fabric. It may be made from cotton, linen, silk or synthetics. Traditionally used for table linens, upholstery and draperies, light and medium weight damask can be used for special occasion garments. As fabric fibre content varies, test pleat a sample before beginning a project. Launder according to the manufacturer's instructions.

Drill

A sturdy, twill weave, medium to heavy weight fabric, usually made of cotton or cotton blends. It is often used for work clothes or uniforms. Test pleat to determine suitability. It can be machine washed.

Georgette

A sheer lightweight fabric made with a crêpe thread often of silk or synthetic fibres. It is very similar in appearance to chiffon and is commonly used for dresses, blouses and lingerie.

It can be difficult to pleat, due to the nature of the fabric. Gentle machine or handwash synthetic georgette - silk should be drycleaned.

Gingham

Elspeth, AS&E 25

This is a closely woven, light to medium weight, plain weave fabric using a dyed warp thread. At least two colours are used to produce a checked appearance. Most often, cotton or cotton blend fibres are used.

Gingham pleats easily with a pleater but is often pleated by hand to achieve a uniform appearance. Gentle machine or hand washing is recommended.

Knits

Beach Baby, AS&E 50

This includes fabrics made by loops joining loops in successive rows. There are a number of different types of knit fabrics in various weights and fibre types, from fine interlock knits to heavy weight rugby. Velour knits have a rich, napped surface. Take care not to stretch the fabric when feeding through the pleater.

Printed fabrics may prove difficult to pleat depending on the medium used for the print. Knit fabrics are very comfortable to wear due to their elastic nature. Fine or medium weight fabrics are most suited to smocking. Gentle machine or hand washing is recommended.

Lace

A decorated cotton or synthetic fibre fabric often made on a background of net or with no background fabric at all, commonly with floral or geometric motifs in the design. There are many different types of lace from very fine, sheer fabrics, to those that are heavy and ornately patterned. The fabric can be made by hand or machine. Fine laces with relatively open designs pleat easily. Laundering requirements may vary from handwashing to drycleaning depending upon the delicacy and composition of the lace fabric used.

Lawn

Faraway Thoughts, AS&E 38

A moderately lightweight, opaque plain weave fabric originally made from linen, but usually made today from combed cotton or cotton blends and synthetic fibres. It has a crisp, crease resistant finish. Lawn is slightly heavier than batiste but can be used for similar purposes. It can be difficult to pleat if densely woven, eg. Liberty Tana lawn. Gentle machine or handwash.

Linen

This fabric is manufactured from the flax plant. It is made in various weights for different purposes. Handkerchief linen is a fine, sheer fabric used for clothing and is beautifully comfortable to wear. Linen fabrics usually pleat easily. Linen has a high shrinkage rate and should be pre-washed before beginning a garment. It may be laundered by hand or machine, or drycleaned if required. Linen will require a hot steam iron due to its tendency to crease easily.

Net

Fabric that is constructed by knotting and looping a continuous thread into an open mesh. It may be composed of cotton or synthetic fibres. It has a stiff texture and is often used to support other fabrics in areas such as puffed sleeves or skirts. Care will vary depending on the fibre composition, so follow the manufacturer's advice.

Organdy/Organza

Tinkerbelle, AS&E 30

Originally, organdy was a sheer, lightweight, cotton fabric with a stiff finish. The same fabric made of silk was referred to as organza. The two names are now interchangeable and these fabrics are also manufactured with synthetic fibres. It is used for special occasion garments and pleats easily. Drycleaning is recommended.

Piqué

My Pretty Maid, AS&E 48

A crisp, medium to heavy weight fabric woven with small, raised geometric patterns, usually made of cotton or cotton/synthetic blends. White piqué is often used for collars and cuffs on dresses and blouses but can be used for whole garments. It can be pleated easily. Gentle machine or handwash.

Poplin

A plain weave fabric with much more warp yarn than weft, and it has a characteristic warp rib appearance. It is best recognised as shirting fabric and may be composed of cotton, synthetics or blends. Due to its densely woven nature, poplin can be difficult to pleat. Warm hand or machine washing is recommended.

Ramie

This name refers to a fibre from the nettle or Urtica family of plants mainly grown in China, Indonesia, Taiwan and Japan. It is sometimes blended with cotton for the manufacture of less expensive clothing and is often confused with linen. Its pleatability and care are similar to linen but if blended with other fibres, the care instructions will alter to cater for those.

Sateen

A strong, lustrous, satin weave fabric made of cotton as distinguished from other satin weave fabrics made of silk or synthetic fibres. It drapes beautifully and is suitable for gowns, blouses and lingerie. Pleatability may vary depending on the density and weight of the fabric. Densely woven fabrics will be difficult to pleat. Drycleaning is recommended.

Satin

Liquid Gold, AS&E 58

Refers to fabrics made using another basic weave pattern, characterized by smooth, lustrous surfaces with longer warp threads 'floating' over the top of the weft threads. This produces a beautiful fabric, made of either silk or synthetic threads. It is made in a variety of weights and can be shiny on one side or both.

Satin is most often used for special occasion garments or lingerie. Its pleatability can vary from easy to difficult depending on the thickness of the fabric and the fibres used. Usually, natural fibre satins will pleat more easily than synthetic satins. When in doubt, test pleat the fabric. Satin fabrics are often easily bruised, so dryclean natural fibres and handwash synthetics.

Seersucker

The Happy Child, AS&E 55

A fabric usually of cotton, cotton blends or nylon. It is made to have a crinkled effect in the lengthwise direction by holding some threads tightly and other threads loosely during the weaving process. Seersucker effects are not lost during laundering and wear. It is easy to pleat and can be hand or gently machine washed.

Silk Dupion

The Little Flowergirl, AS&E 39

Also known as dupioni, this is a lustrous, papery silk fabric made from fibres of silk worm cocoons in which two worms have nested together, creating a double fibre. The resulting fabric has an irregular texture with characteristic 'slubs'. A luxury fabric often used for special occasion garments, silk dupion pleats moderately easily, but sometimes pleats have a tendency to 'pop' after pleating and can be difficult to restore. Packing the pleats tightly and steaming before smocking may help prevent this. As with most silks, the recommended care is drycleaning.

Silk Fuji

A fine, soft, plain weave silk fabric with beautiful draping qualities. It is ideal for special occasion garments and pleats easily. It should only be dry-cleaned to maintain fabric finish.

Specialty Fabrics

Mint Julep, AS&E 24

Fabrics with surface detail such as flocking, embroidery or beading, require special preparation to allow them to be pleated successfully.

Flocked fabrics can be pleated with the needles avoiding the spots or the spots can be removed from the area to be smocked before pleating.

Beaded fabrics must have the beads removed before the fabric is put through the pleater. These can be re-attached after the smocking is complete.

Embroidered fabrics may be pleated if the embroidered surface is not too thick for the pleater needles to go through. Test pleat a sample to determine suitability.

Taffeta

A plain weave, crisp fabric with a lustrous surface and characteristic rustling sound, originally made of silk but now also made of synthetic fibres. It is often used for special occasion garments and

is manufactured in a variety of types. Moiré and paper taffeta are two examples. Pleatability may vary depending on the weight, composition and density of the fabric. Test pleat a sample to determine suitability. Drycleaning is recommended.

Tulle

Princess Charming, AS&E 58

A very fine net, formerly made only of silk, tulle is now also made of cotton and nylon and is a favourite for bridal veils. It may be used as an overlay and pleated together with another fabric such as silk. Pleat slowly and carefully to avoid bent and broken needles. Care will vary depending on the fibre composition, so follow the manufacturer's advice.

Twill

A twill fabric refers to one of the three basic fabric weave patterns and is characterised by its diagonal line effect. It includes many easily recognisable fabrics, such as gaberdine, denim, some flannel fabrics and many others. A twill weave is often used for winter weight garments. Some twills are brushed on the wrong side to create a soft, napped surface. Fine twill fabrics are commonly used for smocked garments and pleat easily. The fibre used in twill fabrics varies, so the care instructions from the manufacturer should be followed.

Velvet

Lily May, AS&E 29

This is a medium weight, woven fabric with a short, dense pile. Originally made of silk, it is now made of many different fibres and is usually regarded as a luxury fabric for special occasion garments. There are a number of different varieties of velvet derived from various treatments to the pile in manufacture. Good quality velvet is usually not difficult to pleat, however, test pleating a sample before beginning a project is recommended. Follow pattern layouts according to 'with nap' instructions and place pins into the seam allowances only to avoid damaging the surface. Position pins close together to

prevent the fabric layers from 'walking' on one another. Finger press seams. If necessary, carefully steam press on the wrong side without touching the fabric surface. Ironing directly on the fabric can cause irreparable damage to the pile. To raise a flattened surface, hang the garment in a steamy room and brush the pile with a velvet brush. Velvet should always be drycleaned.

Velveteen

Velveteen differs from velvet in that the pile in velvet is made with the warp threads, while the pile in velveteen is made with the filling or weft threads. Its characteristics are otherwise similar to velvet and it is manufactured from the same range of fibres, so should be treated in a similar manner.

Voile

Cupcake, AS&E 54

A sheer, lightweight, plain weave fabric made from tightly twisted yarns in a high yarn count construction, the warp of which is

two-ply. Voile drapes beautifully, is similar in appearance to organdy and organza and is easy to pleat. It is commonly composed of cotton, polyester, a combination of both fibres, or silk. Pure cotton voile creases easily whereas cotton blends do not. Voile is often used for infant wear, lingerie and blouses. Cotton or cotton blends may be handwashed. Silk voile should only be drycleaned.

Wool Flannel

Bright Eyes, AS&E 51

A warm, soft, medium to heavyweight fabric composed of tightly woven twill or plain weave and finished with a light napping on the front, back or both sides of the fabric. Medium weight wool flannel can be used for clothing, whereas blankets are examples of heavy weight flannel. Used in smocking, medium weight wool flannel usually pleats easily. Drycleaning is recommended to minimise shrinkage.

FABRIC REQUIREMENTS

BASIC SQUARE YOKE FABRIC REQUIREMENTS

Garment:
Plain calf length skirt, sash, short puffed sleeves with bands and Peter Pan collar.

Size	Requirements 112cm (44") wide	
3 months (no sash)	1.6m	1yd 27"
6 months (no sash)	1.7m	1yd 31"
12 months (no sash)	1.8m	1yd 35"
18 months	2.1m	2yd 10 3/4"
2 years	2.2m	2yd 14 5/8"
3 years	2.4m	2yd 22 1/2"
4 years	2.6m	2yd 30 3/8"
5 years	2.7m	2yd 34 1/4"
6 years	2.8m	3yd 2 1/4"
7 years	2.9m	3yd 6 1/4"
8 years	3.0m	3yd 10"
9 years	3.1m	3yd 14"
10 years	3.2m	3yd 18"

Note: for long sleeves add 20cm (8") for each size.

Garment:
Plain calf length skirt, sash and short puffed sleeves with contrasting Peter Pan collar and sleeves bands.

Size	Requirements 112cm (44") wide	
3 months (no sash)	1.4m	1yd 19"
6 months (no sash)	1.5m	1yd 23"
12 months (no sash)	1.6m	1yd 27"
18 months	1.9m	2yd 4 3/4"
2 years	2.0m	2yd 6 3/4"
3 years	2.2m	2yd 14 5/8"
4 years	2.4m	2yd 22 1/2"
5 years	2.5m	2yd 26 1/2"
6 years	2.6m	2yd 30 3/8"
7 years	2.7m	2yd 34 1/4"
8 years	2.8m	3yd 2 1/4"
9 years	2.9m	3yd 6 1/4"
10 years	3.0m	3yd 10"

Note: for long sleeves add 20cm (8") for each size. The contrast collar and cuffs require an additional 25cm (10") for each size.

BISHOP FABRIC REQUIREMENTS

Garment: Plain calf length skirt and short puffed sleeves with sleeve bands.

Size	Requirements 112cm (44") wide		Size	Requirements 112cm (44") wide	
3 months	1.5m	1yd 23"	2 years	2.0m	2yd 6 3/4"
6 months	1.6m	1yd 27"	3 years	2.2m	2yd 14 5/8"
12 months	1.8m	1yd 35"	4 years	2.4m	2yd 22 1/2"
18 months	1.9m	2yd 4 3/4"	5 years	2.6m	2yd 30 3/8"

Note: for long sleeves add 20cm (8") for each size.

INTERFACINGS AND INTERLININGS

Interfacings and interlinings are used to stiffen, stabilize, strengthen and support some elements of a smocked garment, particularly collars, cuffs and button bands. The entire front yoke and back bodice pieces can be interfaced if the fabric has 'show through'. This prevents the seams from being visible.

Fusible interfacing can also be used to stabilize a smocked piece before cutting out. This prevents the smocked surface from stretching when the garment is constructed.

Interfacings, fusible or non-fusible, woven or non-woven, come in a range of weights. Fusible interfacings are often chosen for their ease of use, but they are unsuitable for napped fabrics such as velvet or velveteen and any fabric that would be damaged by the heat and pressure of fusing. When buying fusible interfacing, ask for instructions for fusing it correctly. These are often supplied by the manufacturer. Take special note of the iron setting and time required. Use a pressing cloth to protect the fabric if necessary. Ensure the fusible side of the interfacing is facing the fabric, not the iron, before pressing.

Interlinings are used when soft support, rather than stiffness, is required or if the fabric is transparent. An interlining is often made from the same fabric as the garment. The layers of fabric are tacked together and subsequently treated as one.

MACHINE SEWING THREAD

Choosing the correct thread for constructing a garment is just as important as choosing the fabric and smocking design. Machine threads are available in various fibres and weights from extra fine (100) pure cotton to heavy (30) cotton or polyester topstitching threads.

Cotton thread is numbered to indicate the thickness (80, 60, 50, 30) and if there is a second number (60/2), this indicates the number of plies used to make the thread - in this case, two.

Polyester thread uses a different sizing system, 100 polyester is not as fine as 100 cotton, but the higher the number, the finer the thread.

Always buy the best quality thread available and store it away from sunlight and protected from dust and insects.

There are threads especially for fine or heirloom sewing. Fine weight threads make stitches that are less visible on fine fabrics. Pure cotton is a weaker fibre than polyester. Better quality cotton threads are made using long staple Egyptian cotton and the thread can be mercerised to increase its strength and lustre.

Good quality long staple polyester thread can be used for most tasks and it is available in a variety of different finishes.

PATTERNS

Determine the correct pattern by taking the relevant measurements and comparing them with those on the standard sizing chart. Very few children will fit the sizing for their age exactly. Use the size that best fits your child's chest measurement. You may need to make alterations to the length of the garment. Carefully trace the pattern onto tracing paper or lightweight interfacing including all pattern markings. Accuracy is very important to ensure the proper fit of the garment. If changing the number of smocking rows from that specified in the pattern, you will need to adjust the length of the back bodice to ensure that the lowest row of smocking lines up with the back bodice/skirt seam.

STANDARD BODY MEASUREMENTS FOR CHILDREN (AUSTRALIA)

Size	Newborn	3m	6m	12m	18m	2yr	3yr
Height	56cm (22")	62cm (24 3/8")	68cm (26 3/4")	76cm (30")	84cm (33")	92cm (36 1/4")	100cm (39 5/8")
Weight	4kg (8 1/2 lb)	6kg (12 3/4 lb)	8kg (17lb)	10kg (21 1/4 lb)	12kg (25 1/2 lb)	-	-
Chest	41cm (16 1/8")	44cm (17 1/4")	47cm (18 1/2")	50cm (19 1/4")	53cm (20 7/8")	56cm (22")	58cm (22 3/4")
Waist	41cm (16 1/8")	44cm (17 1/4")	47cm (18 1/2")	50cm (19 1/4")	52cm (20 1/2")	54cm (21 1/4")	55cm (21 5/8")
Hip	-	-	-	-	52cm (20 1/2")	56cm (22")	59cm (23 1/4")
Back length (nape to waist)	15cm (6")	16cm (6 1/4")	17cm (6 3/4")	19cm (7 1/2")	21cm (8 1/4")	23cm (9")	25cm (9 3/4")

Size	4yr	5yr	6yr	7yr	8yr	9yr	10yr
Height	108cm (41 1/2")	115cm (45 1/4")	120cm (47 1/4")	125cm (49 1/4")	130cm (51 1/4")	135cm (53 1/8")	140cm (55 1/8")
Chest	60cm (23 5/8")	62cm (24 3/8")	64cm (25 1/8")	66cm (26")	68cm (26 3/4")	71cm (28")	74cm (29 1/8")
Waist	56cm (22")	57cm (22 3/8")	58cm (22 3/4")	59cm (23 1/4")	60cm (23 5/8")	61cm (24")	62cm (24 3/8")
Hip	62cm (24 3/8")	64cm (25 1/8")	66cm (26")	68cm (26 3/4")	72cm (28 3/8")	75cm (29 1/2")	78cm (30 3/4")
Back length (nape to waist)	26cm (10 1/4")	27cm (10 5/8")	28cm (11")	29cm (11 3/8")	29cm (11 3/8")	30cm (12")	31cm (12 1/4")

STANDARD BODY MEASUREMENTS FOR CHILDREN (USA)

Size	Newborn	6m	1yr	2yr	3yr	
Height	24"	28"	31"	35"	38"	
Weight	13lb	18lb	-	-	-	
Chest	18"	19"	20"	21"	22"	
Waist	18"	19"	19 1/2"	20"	20 1/2"	
Hip	19"	20"	21"	22"	23"	
Back length (nape to waist)	6 1/8"	7 1/2"	8"	8 1/2"	9"	
Size	4yr	5yr	6yr	7yr	8yr	10yr
Height	41"	44"	47"	50"	52"	56"
Chest	23"	24"	25"	26"	27"	28 1/8"
Waist	21"	21 1/2"	22"	23"	23 1/2"	24 1/2"
Hip	24"	25"	26"	27"	28"	30"
Back length (nape to waist)	9 1/2"	10"	10 1/2"	11 1/2"	12"	12 3/4"

CUTTING LAYOUT

The cutting layout is designed so that all the required pieces of the garment can be cut in the most economical way and on the correct grainline.

Take special care to note whether the fabric is cut on the fold or as a single layer. Pattern pieces that need to be mirror imaged before cutting are indicated on the cutting layout.

PINNING THE PATTERN TO THE FABRIC

Press the fabric to remove all creases. Lay the fabric on a flat surface. Fold with right sides together and the selvedges parallel. Following the cutting layout, pin the pattern pieces in place. When cutting plaids, stripes and spots on the fold, ensure that both fabric layers are properly aligned.

CUTTING OUT

Accuracy in cutting is important to ensure that all pattern pieces are accurately cut out so they fit together correctly. Use good quality, sharp dressmaking scissors and cut with the scissors held at a right angle to the fabric. Use the full blade as this ensures a straight cut edge. Fabrics that fray excessively should have the cut edges neatened.

TRANSFERRING MARKINGS

Transfer pattern markings onto the fabric using one of the following methods.

TAILOR'S TACKS

Tailor's tacks are the traditional method for transferring markings onto fabric. Use thread in a contrasting colour.

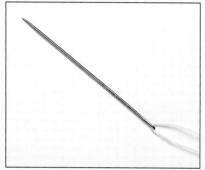

1. Thread the needle with a double length of thread.

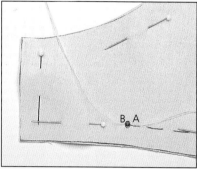

2. Take the thread to the back at A leaving a 3cm (1 1/8") tail. Emerge at B.

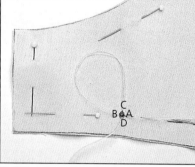

3. Take thread to back at C, leaving a 6cm (2 1/2") loop. Emerge at D.

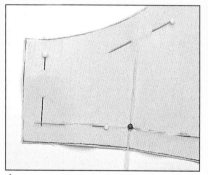

4. Leaving a 3cm (1 1/8") tail, cut the thread and loop.

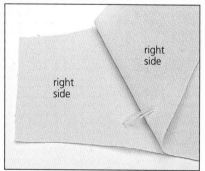

5. Separate the fabric layers.

6. Cut the threads.

MARKING SEAMLINES

To mark seamlines, unthread your sewing machine and stitch a line at the seamline. The needle will leave a row of small holes indicating the seamline position.

WATER-SOLUBLE AND FADE-AWAY MARKERS

Make a small hole through the pattern piece at the marked point. Make a mark through the hole. Push a pin though both layers of fabric at the marked point. Mark the second side.

TAILOR'S PENCIL AND CHALK

Suitable for dark fabrics, use these in the same way as the markers.

TECHNIQUES

BINDING

A binding is used to neaten a raw edge on a garment and can be a single or double (French) binding. A double binding is not suitable for thick fabrics. When using a pattern not specifically designed with bound edges, it is necessary to trim away all the garment seam allowance before attaching the binding to ensure a correct fit.

SINGLE BINDING METHOD 1

To determine the measurement for the width of the bias strip, decide on the finished width and multiply by four. For example, to achieve a finished binding 6mm (1/4") wide, cut the bias strip 24mm (1") wide.

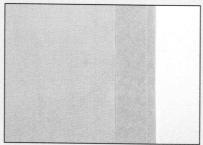

1. With right sides together and matching raw edges, pin and stitch the binding in place 6mm (1/4") from the raw edge.

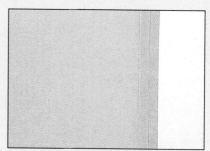

2. Press the binding towards the seam allowance. Fold the binding so the raw edge butts the raw edge of the seam allowance. Press.

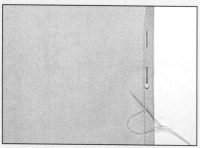

3. Fold the pressed edge, enclosing the seam allowance. Hand stitch in place along the previous stitchline.

SINGLE BINDING METHOD 2

To determine the measurement for the width of the bias strip, decide on the finished width and multiply by five. For example, to achieve a finished binding 6mm (1/4") wide, cut the bias strip 30mm (1 1/4") wide.

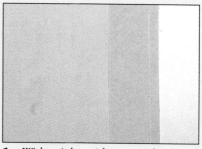

1. With right sides together and matching raw edges, pin and stitch the binding in place 6mm (1/4") from the raw edge.

2. Fold the binding so that the remaining long edge meets the stitchline.

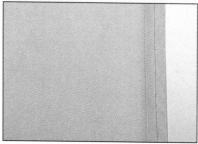

3. Fold the seam allowance back onto the folded binding.

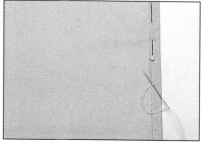

4. Fold the binding, enclosing the seam allowance. Hand stitch in place along the previous stitchline.

DOUBLE (FRENCH) BINDING

To determine the measurement for the width of the bias strip, decide on the finished width and multiply by six.
For example, to achieve a finished binding 6mm (1/4") wide, cut the bias strip 36mm (1 1/2") wide.

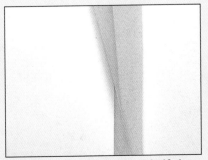

1. Fold the binding strip in half along the length and press.

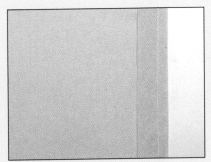

2. With right sides together and matching raw edges, pin and stitch in place 6mm (1/4") from the raw edge.

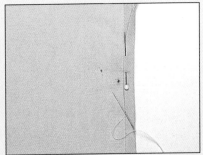

3. Fold the binding, enclosing the seam allowance. Hand stitch in place along the previous stitchline.

BLOCKING AND SHAPING

Before working the smocking, the pleated fabric is tied off to fit the blocking guide that is supplied with most patterns specifically designed for smocking. After working the smocking the width of the smocked panel may be less than it was tied off to. The fabric must be blocked to re-establish the correct width.

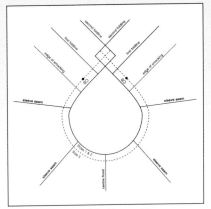

Bishop blocking guide

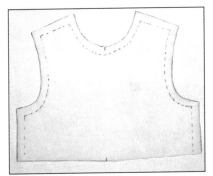

Full bodice blocking guide

Square yoke blocking guide

Baby Blue, AS&E 47

SQUARE YOKE GARMENT

1. Remove the pleating threads, except for the holding rows. Place the panel face up on a padded board. Pin the panel at the top and bottom of the centre front.

2. Place the blocking guide over the panel, matching centres and the upper stitchline. Pin the panel to the board, stretching it to match the guide. Pin frequently.

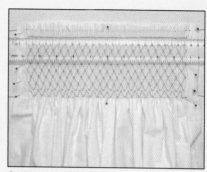

3. Remove the blocking guide. Using a ruler, check that the rows of smocking are straight and the pleats are evenly distributed.

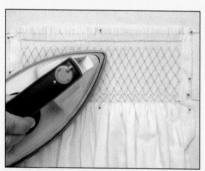

4. Steam the smocking by holding a steam iron approx. 2.5cm (1") above the panel. Alternatively, dampen by spraying with a water atomiser.

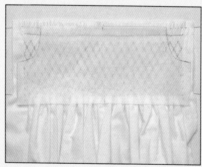

5. Leave the panel pinned until completely dry. Remove the pins and place the blocking guide over the panel, positioning it as before.

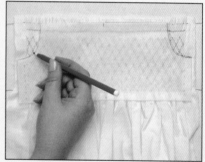

6. Mark the armhole shaping with a fabric marker or lead pencil. Remove the blocking guide.

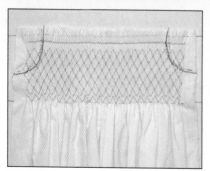

7. Stitch with a tiny zigzag or straight stitch 2 - 3mm (⅛") inside the marked lines to secure the smocking. Do not stretch the panel or flatten the pleats as you stitch.

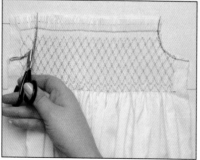

8. Carefully cut out along the marked shaping lines.

9. Completed blocked and shaped smocked skirt ready to assemble.

FULL BODICE GARMENT **METHOD 1**

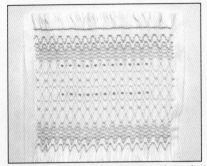

1. Remove all the pleating threads. Place the smocked panel face up on a padded board.

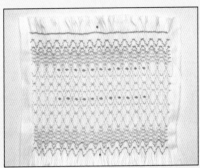

2. Pin the panel to the board at the top and bottom of the centre front.

3. Place the blocking guide over the panel, matching centres and the last row of smocking. Pin the panel, matching the sides to the guide.

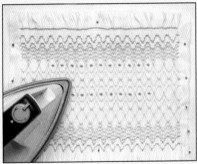

4. Remove the blocking guide. Steam the smocking by holding a steam iron approx. 2.5cm (1") above the panel or spray with an atomiser.

5. Leave the panel pinned until dry. Remove the pins and place the blocking guide over the panel, positioning it as before.

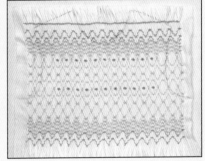

6. Mark the armhole, neck and shoulder shaping with a fabric marker or lead pencil. Remove the blocking guide.

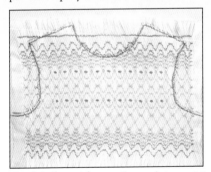

7. Stitch with a tiny zigzag or straight stitch 2 - 3mm (⅛") inside the marked lines to secure the smocking. Do not stretch the panel or flatten the pleats as you stitch.

8. Carefully cut out along the marked shaping lines.

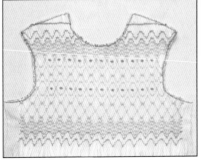

9. Completed blocked and shaped smocked bodice ready to assemble.

FULL BODICE GARMENT **METHOD 2**

1. Remove all the pleating threads. Place the smocked panel face up on a padded board.

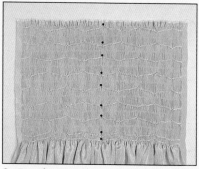

2. Pin the panel to the board along the centre front.

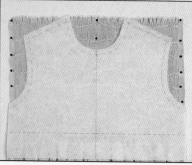

3. Place the blocking guide over the panel, matching centres. Adjust the panel to fit the guide. Pin in place along the sides.

4. Remove the blocking guide. Steam the smocking by holding a steam iron approx. 2.5cm (1") above the panel or spray with an atomiser.

5. Leave the panel pinned until dry. Remove the pins and place the panel face down on the padded board.

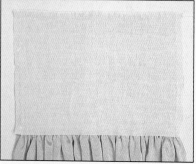

6. Matching the upper and side edges, place a rectangle of woven fusible interfacing, fusible side down, on the panel. Lightly press to fuse.

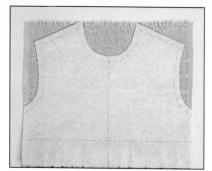

7. Matching centres, reposition the blocking guide on the right side of the panel. Mark the shaping with a fabric marker.

8. Carefully cut out along the marked shaping lines. The fused interfacing will stabilise the panel.

9. Completed blocked and shaped smocked bodice ready to assemble.

BISHOP GARMENT

A bishop garment should be blocked before and after smocking to ensure the correct shaping.

Cherry Surprise, AS&E 42

1. Unpick the pleating threads at the centre back or front opening according to the pattern directions.

2. Place the blocking guide on a padded flat surface such as an ironing board.

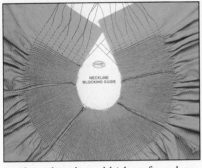

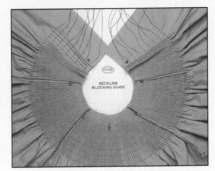

3. Place the pleated bishop face down on the blocking guide. Fan out the pleats and match the raw edge at the neckline with the guideline for the required size.

4. Matching the seams and centre front or back to the corresponding lines on the guide, pin the neckline in place.

5. Just beyond the lower edge of the pleating, pin the seams and centre back or front opening to the corresponding lines on the guide.

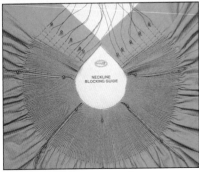

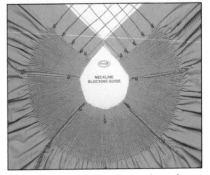

6. Matching the first pleat positions on the guide, pin the back or front opening edges in place.

7. Distribute the pleats evenly. Leaving the upper holding row free, tie off the remaining pleating threads in pairs along one back or front opening edge.

8. Firmly tie off the same threads on the other side. Steam or spray starch the pleats to help hold them in place. Allow to dry before unpinning.

GATHERING

Gathering is a way of softly controlling fullness in fabric.

GATHERING WITH A SEWING MACHINE

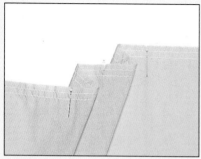

1. Divide the piece into quarters and mark with pins. Using a long straight stitch, stitch a row of machine gathering along each side of the stitchline.

2. Pull up the gathering threads until the piece is approximately the same width as the flat piece.

3. With right sides together and matching quarter marks, pin to the corresponding piece. Distribute the gathers evenly. Remove marking pins.

4. Wrap the thread around the end pins in a figure eight to prevent the threads from slipping.

5. Set the machine stitch length to normal. Stitch the seam along the stitchline, between the gathering rows.

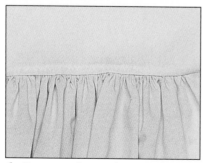

6. Remove the gathering threads. Trim and neaten the seam.

SUCCESSFUL GATHERING

1. Use a long straight stitch.

2. Stitch the gathering rows with the right side of the fabric facing up. This means that the bobbin threads will face you when stitching the gathered piece to a flat piece.

3. Slightly loosening the needle thread tension will make it easier to pull up the gathers and also to remove the gathering threads.

4. Use a different colour thread in the bobbin to help identify it.

5. Always pull up the bobbin threads.

6. Stitch the gathering rows each side of the stitchline - they are easier to remove this way.

7. When gathering long pieces, break the stitching at seams or centres and pull up the gathers in sections.

8. Divide the piece to be gathered into halves or quarters and mark with pins. Divide the flat piece and mark in the same way. Match the pins when attaching the pieces.

GATHERING WITH A SMOCKING PLEATER

If very even gathers are required, a smocking pleater will produce small, evenly spaced pleats.

The First Communion, AS&E 58

The Magic Flute, AS&E 61

Daisy Mae, AS&E 62

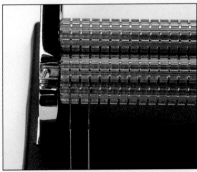

1. Thread two full space pleater needles with thread that contrasts with the fabric.

2. Roll the back skirt onto the pleating rod and position it behind the pleater with the top raw edge 5mm (3/16") from the first pleating row.

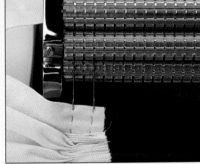

3. Pleat the first half of the skirt, clearing the fabric from the needles at the centre back placket. Do not allow the placket to overlap itself as it goes through the pleater.

4. Pleat the second half of the skirt. Remove the fabric from the pleater.

5. Adjust the pleating threads and cut at the centre back.

6. Unpick the threads that fall within the placket for 1cm (3/8") at the sides.

7. Tie off the threads on the wrong side to fit the back yokes or bodice pieces.

HEIRLOOM SEWING

Heirloom sewing refers to those techniques traditionally used in the making of fine garments.
In the past these techniques were done by hand but many of them can now be done with a sewing machine.

JOINING FLAT LACE TO FLAT FABRIC

Rolling and whipping is a term borrowed from French hand sewing to describe the machine
heirloom sewing technique shown here. Rolling and whipping gives a firm but dainty seam.
To be successful, the zigzag stitch used should be slightly wider than the distance between the lace
heading and the raw edge of the fabric. The needle must not pierce the fabric, but swing right
off the edge. This allows the raw edge to curl into the seam, thus forming the 'roll'.
The stitch length should be relatively short, but not as short as satin stitch.
Use a fine machine sewing thread that matches the lace, rather than the fabric colour.

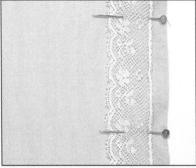

1. With right sides together and with the lace heading along the stitchline, pin the lace to the fabric.

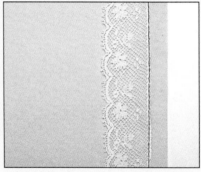

2. Stitch along the centre of the heading with a short straight stitch.

3. Trim the raw edge of the fabric to within 3mm ($1/8''$) of the lace heading.

4. Begin the wide close zigzag stitching.

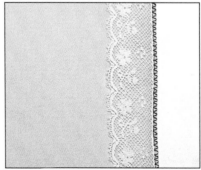

5. Continue the zigzag. The seam will roll into the stitching.

6. Press the seam towards the fabric and the lace away from the fabric.

JOINING GATHERED LACE TO FLAT FABRIC

Place a pin at the centre of the lace and at the centre of the flat fabric. Stitch a machine or hand gathering thread or pull the gimp thread in the heading of the lace and gather to fit the flat fabric. Distribute the gathers evenly.

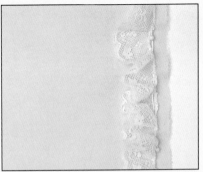

1. With right sides together, matching centre pins and the lace uppermost, pin so the heading lies as flat as possible against the fabric along the stitchline.

2. Follow steps 2 - 6 for joining lace to flat fabric.

JOINING ENTREDEUX TO FLAT FABRIC

Check the entredeux carefully to ensure that you are using the correct side. The stitching will appear smoother on the right side.

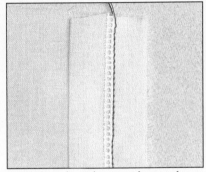

1. With right sides together and raw edges even, place the untrimmed heading of the entredeux onto the fabric. Using a short stitch length 'stitch in the ditch' of the entredeux.

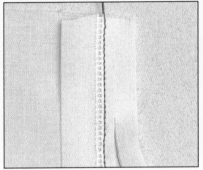

2. Trim the seam to approximately 3mm (1/8") as evenly as possible to ensure a straight seam. Ensure there are no 'whiskers' on the trimmed edge.

3. Stitch, using a zigzag stitch slightly longer than satin stitch. The stitch width should align with the previous straight stitching on the left and just clear the raw edge of the fabric on the right.

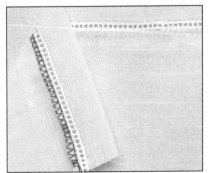

4. Press the seam towards the fabric and the entredeux away.

Milestones, AS&E 43

JOINING ENTREDEUX TO GATHERED FABRIC

Entredeux is a French term meaning 'between two'.
This dainty trim is commonly used when joining lace to fabric, lace to lace or in garment seams.

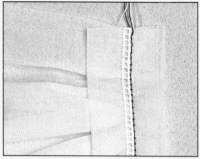

1. With wrong sides together and raw edges even, pin the untrimmed entredeux to the gathered fabric. Using a straight stitch, 'stitch in the ditch' of the entredeux.

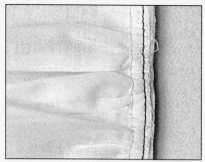

2. Trim the seam ensuring the fabric allowance is slightly narrower than the entredeux. This allows the entredeux heading to roll over the fabric. Stitch with the fabric side up.

3. Stitch, with a zigzag stitch slightly longer than satin stitch. The stitch width should align with the straight stitching on the left and just clear the raw edge of the entredeux on the right.

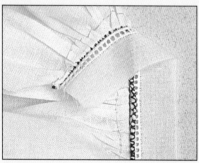

4. Press the seam towards the fabric and the entredeux away. **Completed rolled and whipped entredeux to gathered fabric.**

JOINING FLAT LACE TO ENTREDEUX

Take care not to cut the stitching on the entredeux when trimming away the fabric heading.

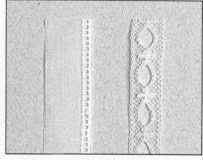

1. Trim away the heading from one side of the entredeux.

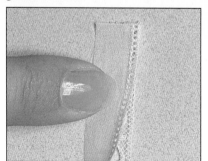

2. With right sides together, place the trimmed edge of the entredeux over the edge of the lace heading and pin.

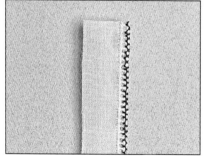

3. Adjust the zigzag stitch so the needle goes into each hole of the entredeux and swings wide enough to just clear the lace heading. Stitch.

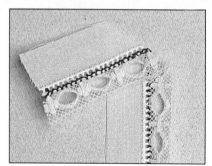

4. Press the lace and entredeux open.

INSERTING LACE

Using a fabric marker or pencil, mark guidelines on the fabric
for the position of the lace insertion.

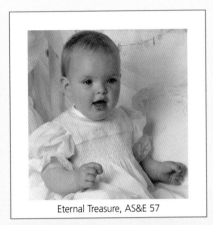

Eternal Treasure, AS&E 57

1. With the right side facing up, lay a length of lace insertion between the marked guidelines.

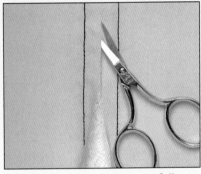

2. Pin and tack the lace in place, inside the lace heading.

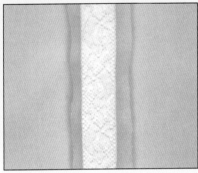

3. Stitch along both edges of the lace heading using a small straight machine stitch. Remove the tacking.

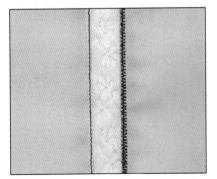

4. Separating the layers, carefully cut the fabric along the centre behind the lace.

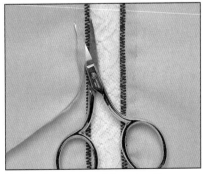

5. On the wrong side, press the seam allowance away from the lace.

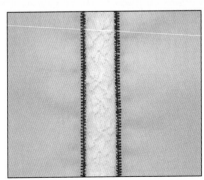

6. On the right side, zigzag over the previous stitching.

7. On the wrong side, trim the seam allowance close to the zigzag stitching.

8. Remove any visible guidelines. Press.

LACE EDGED SCALLOPS

Unless otherwise specified, use heirloom machine sewing thread and a fine machine
needle (size 60 - 70). Mark the scallops onto the fabric using a water-soluble marker or lead pencil.
If the lace has no gimp thread, run a row of machine or hand gathering along the lace heading.

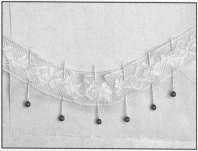

1. Beginning at one side seam and leaving a 2.5cm (1") tail, pin the lower edge of the lace insertion to the traced scallop line as shown. Pin to the peak of the first scallop.

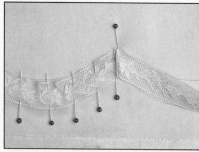

2. Pin the upper edge of the lace at the peak.

3. Position the lace along the next scallop. A pleat will form on the lower line. Mark the lower edge of the lace on each side of the pleat at the peak.

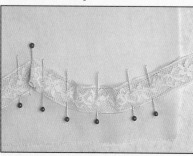

4. Continue positioning the lace in the same manner around the hem. When reaching the starting point, trim the lace, leaving a 2.5cm (1") tail.

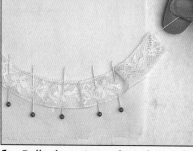

5. Pull the gimp thread in the heading of the upper edge of the lace so that it lies flat along the upper curve.

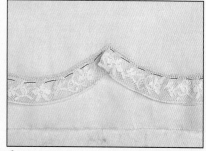

6. Tack. Using a tiny zigzag no wider than the lace heading, stitch along the upper lace edge keeping the pleat free.

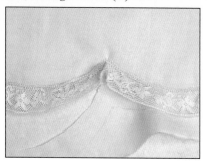

7. With the wrong side uppermost, trim the fabric away from behind the lace, close to the zigzag stitching, taking care not to cut the lace.

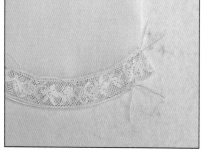

8. Push the lace pleats to the wrong side. Fold the scallop right sides together. Stitch from top to bottom of lace in line with the fold in the fabric.

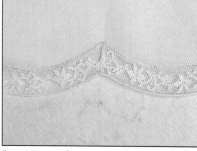

9. Trim close to the stitching. Remove any remaining traces of the fabric marker. Fold out the scallop and press.

LACE INSERTION SCALLOPS

While the instructions below are for inserting scallops into a hemline, the same technique can be used for other lace shapes. Best results are achieved when using a fine sewing machine needle and heirloom sewing thread.

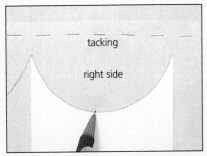

1. Press and spray starch the fabric and the lace insertion. Place a pre-pared template onto the right side of the fabric and draw in the scallops with a fabric marker.

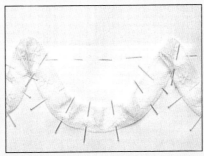

2. Using lace pins, pin the lower edge of the lace insertion along the marked scallop line. Pin frequently approx every 1cm (3/8").

3. Pull the gimp thread in the upper heading of the lace to shape it. Ensure both edges lie flat. (The lace will be folded at the scallop peaks).

4. Using a tiny zigzag, stitch the lower edge of the lace in place.

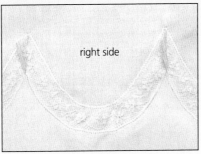

5. Stitch the upper edge of the lace in the same manner. The folds of lace at the peaks are on the right side. Press to ease out any puckers.

6. On the wrong side, trim the fabric away from both edges of the lace close to the stitching. Use small, sharp scissors and cut carefully.

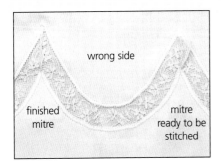

7. Push the folded lace at the peaks through to the wrong side. With right sides together, fold a scallop so the folded lace lies flat. Using a tiny zigzag, stitch through the lace only. Trim the excess lace. Open out the scallop and press.

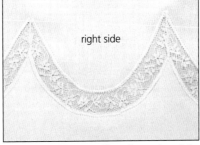

8. Finished lace scallop from the right side. If desired, work pin stitch along both edges of the lace insertion (see page 36).

Sugar and Spice, AS&E 35

MACHINE HEMSTITCH (PIN STITCH)

Hemstitch or 'point de Paris' is a beautiful traditional heirloom technique that can be worked by hand or machine. It can be used for attaching trims, making hems or appliquéing fabric. Use a hemstitch or wing needle when working this technique with a sewing machine.

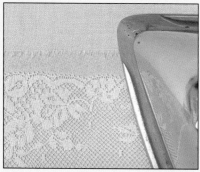

1. Use several light applications of spray starch, pressing between each one, until the fabric and lace are crisp.

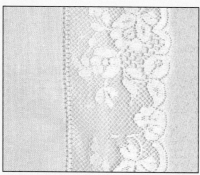

2. With the wrong side of the lace to the right side of the fabric, position the lace heading on the fabric stitchline. Using a fine needle and a tiny zigzag no wider than the lace heading, stitch the lace to the fabric.

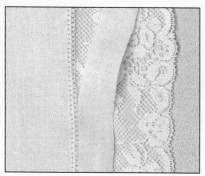

3. Cut the excess fabric from behind the lace, trimming close to the zigzag stitching.

4. Using a suitable hemstitch and needle, stitch so the hemstitch holes lie beside the lace heading in the fabric and the sideways stitches enclose the lace heading.

HINT

Use several light applications of starch, pressing between each one, on the fabric, entredeux and lace before sewing to make them easier to handle.

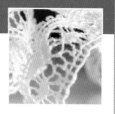

LACES

There are many different types and styles of lace available.

Maline and Valenciennes are fine, delicate laces and are the two types most commonly used for heirloom sewing.

These are usually available in 'families' consisting of insertion, beading and different widths of edging all featuring the same pattern.

When using natural fibre fabrics, choose cotton lace that can withstand the same iron temperature as the fabric. Synthetic lace may melt if pressed with a hot iron.

Many laces have a gimp thread that runs through the heading. This thread looks like a very fine cord. By pulling the gimp thread, the lace can be easily gathered. Laces without a gimp thread need to be gathered by hand or with a sewing machine.

PIPING

MAKING PIPING

Children's garments require a fine gauge piping. Piping is usually made by stitching a narrow cord inside a bias strip of fabric. Wash the piping cord to shrink it before making the piping.

A zipper foot can be useful for stitching close to the cord.

To make fine piping with a 1cm (3/8") heading, cut bias strips 2.5cm (1") wide.

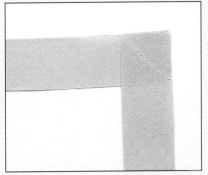

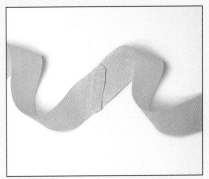

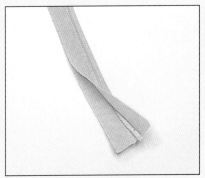

1. Join the bias strips by placing one end of two strips right sides together and at right angles to each other. Stitch diagonally across the overlapping ends.

2. Trim the seam to 6mm (1/4") and press open. Continue joining the strips until you have the desired length of bias.

3. Lay the piping cord along the centre of the bias strip on the wrong side. Fold the fabric over the cord, matching raw edges. Stitch close to the cord.

Country Rose, AS&E 42

REMOVING PIPING CORD

To eliminate excess bulk from seams, remove the piping cord from the seam allowance. Pull 1cm (3/8") of cord out of the end of the bias and trim away.

Pull the fabric firmly to reposition the cord. This allows the piping cord to 'float' within the tube.

Mimosa, AS&E 61

ATTACHING PIPING TO FLAT FABRIC

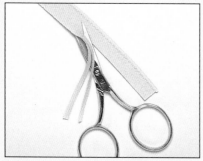

1. Cut a piece of piping the required length. If necessary, trim the piping heading to the same width as the seam allowance.

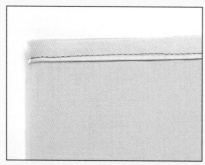

2. Matching raw edges, pin and tack the piping to the right side of the fabric. Stitch along the piping stitchline. Press.

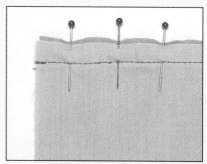

3. With right sides together and matching raw edges, pin the second piece of fabric to the first. The piping is sandwiched between.

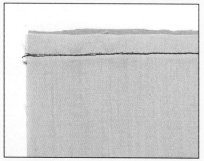

4. With the previous line of stitching uppermost, stitch between the corded edge of the piping and the previous stitchline.

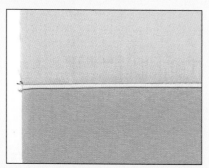

5. Press the stitching. Open out the two layers of fabric and press the seam allowance to one side.

Lilac & Lace, AS&E 66

ATTACHING PIPING TO SMOCKED OR GATHERED FABRIC

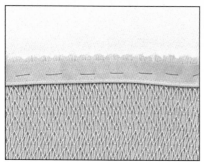

1. Cut a piece of piping the required length. Position the piping so the cord lies just above the top row of smocking or between gathering rows.

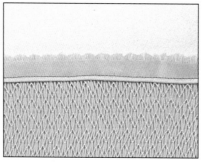

2. Pin and tack the piping to the right side of the fabric. Stitch along the piping stitchline.

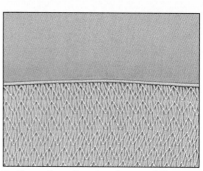

3. Complete the piped seam following steps 3 - 5 above, pressing the seam allowance away from the gathered or smocked fabric.

PLEATING

For most forms of smocking the fabric needs to be pleated before the smocking is worked. The quickest and easiest way to do this is with a smocking pleater, a simple device designed especially for this purpose.

While there are several brands of pleaters available, they all work on the same principle. Four grooved rollers (or gears) are held horizontally between end plates. Curved needles ride in slots between two of the rollers.

As the handle is turned, the gear action draws the fabric in, tucks it into the grooves and forces it onto the needles, then the threads. The result is uniformly pleated fabric.

Needles can be positioned in the pleater to produce rows that are full space, approximately 1cm (3/8") or half space, approximately 5mm (3/16") apart. Fabric can also be pleated using smocking dots that are pinned or ironed onto the fabric. Rows of running stitch are worked uniformly along the dots and the fabric is then drawn up into pleats. Smocking dots are difficult to remove. Test on the fabric that you intend to use.

Similar results can be achieved by marking regularly spaced dots onto fabric with a water-soluble marker or pencil. A bishop garment must be pieced together at the armhole seams before pleating.

Day Dreams, AS&E 36

PLEATING FULL AND HALF SPACE ROWS

Full and half space rows are pleated in the same manner.
The only difference is the spacing between the needles.

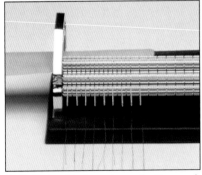

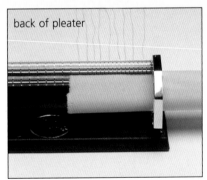

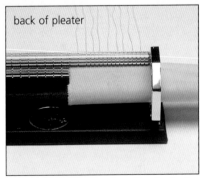

1. Roll the fabric onto a pleating rod. Align the top edge 1cm (3/8") beyond the first threaded needle on the right hand side unless your pattern states otherwise.

2. Place the raw edge of the fabric between the rollers at the back of the pleater. Ensure the fabric is straight.

3. Slowly turn the handle clockwise until you feel the rollers grip the fabric. Ensure the edge of the fabric has caught evenly. If not, reverse the handle and try again.

PLEATING FULL AND HALF SPACE ROWS... CONTINUED

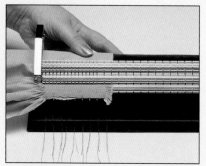

4. Continue turning the handle clockwise until the fabric begins to appear on the needles and the handle becomes a little more difficult to turn.

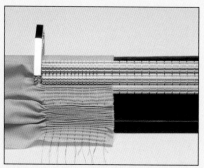

5. Gently ease the pleats off the needles and onto the pleating threads.

6. Continue pleating the fabric, stopping frequently to clear the needles. This reduces stress on the needles, preventing them from bending and eventually breaking.

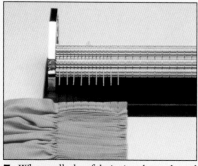

7. When all the fabric is pleated and clear of the rollers, pull it all onto the threads until it is several centimetres away from the ends of the needles.

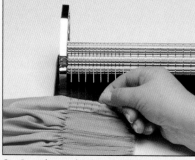

8. Cut through the threads near the ends of the needles or unthread the needles.

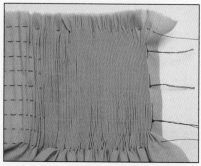

9. Remove the pleating threads from the seam allowances. Leaving the holding rows untied, tie the threads along one side of the fabric in pairs.

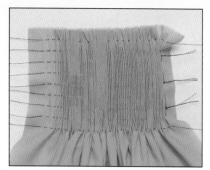

10. Distribute the pleats evenly across the pleating threads to the required width. You can use a fine toothed comb to help straighten the pleats.

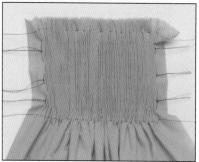

11. Tie off the threads on the remaining side without altering the width of the panel.

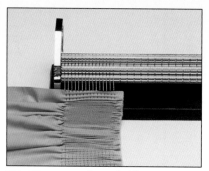

12. Here we show half space rows which are pleated in the same manner as full space rows.

PREPARING AND PLEATING A BISHOP

Before pleating a bishop garment, the front, back and sleeves are stitched together at the armholes. The lower edge of the sleeves can be finished before or after pleating. If finishing after pleating, use pleating threads longer than the width of the flat sleeve. Pleat with the wrong side of the fabric facing you so you can easily check and control the seams.

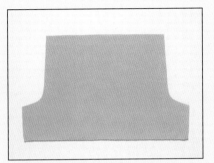

1. Lower sleeve edge. Neaten the raw edge of the lower sleeve using a tiny, close zigzag.

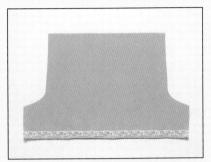

2. With right sides together and the lace heading just inside the neatened edge, place the lace on the fabric. Stitch, using a zigzag covering the entire heading. Press.

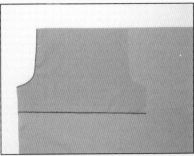

3. Seams. With right sides together, stitch one sleeve to one back piece. Trim the seam to 2 - 3mm (⅛") and neaten. Press.

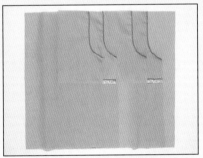

4. Stitch the remaining side of the sleeve to the front. Stitch the second sleeve to the front and back to correspond. Mark the centre front.

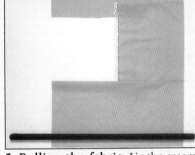

5. Rolling the fabric. Lie the assembled garment wrong side down with the neckline to the right. Place a long pleating rod along the centre back.

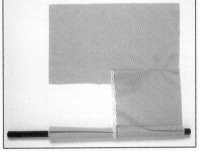

6. Begin rolling the fabric onto the rod slowly and carefully. Ensure the neck edge remains even on the rod for the entire length.

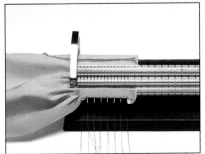

7. Pleating. Thread needles with long threads. Place rod behind the rollers. Align neck edge 1cm (⅜") beyond last needle. Slowly feed fabric through, removing fabric from needles every few turns.

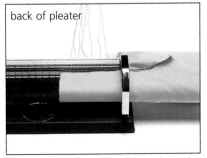

8. Continue pleating until reaching the first seam. Gently pull the fabric off the needles. Turn the handle very slowly, easing the seam through and ensuring it feeds through straight.

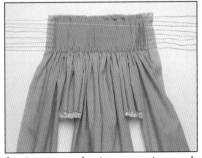

9. Continue pleating, ensuring each seam is parallel to the rollers. Remove the remainder of the fabric from the needles and cut the threads. The bishop is now ready to be blocked.

PRESSING

Pressing is an essential part of good garment construction.
The final finish on a garment owes much to careful pressing.

Always neaten and press a seam before it is crossed with another. Use a good quality spray starch and rinse the nozzle after use to prevent clogging. Allow the starch to soak into the fabric before pressing. This helps to prevent starch buildup on the iron soleplate.

Sequence of pressing a finished garment

Press the sleeves and sleeve bands first, using a sleeve roll or pressing mit to eliminate all creases.

Pack the sleeves with tissue paper or tulle to maintain their shape. Press the collar from the underside. If the collar is embroidered, press into a soft pad. Press the front yoke and back bodices taking care around the buttons. Press the skirt, pushing the iron as far up into the gathers as possible. Finally, press the sashes.

Pressing cloths

Use a pressing cloth to protect the fabric surface when pressing from the right side.

Removing hem creases

Use a Rajah cloth and the iron on a steam setting to eliminate unwanted hem creases.

HINT

Don't press folds into silk unless they are in the perfect position. Pressed folds in silk are extremely difficult to remove.

SEAMS

Old Friends, AS&E 36

Most seams on a smocked garment can be either flat or French (double) seams. Stitch a test seam before beginning a garment to ensure that the machine tension and stitch length are correct.

Use good quality machine sewing thread the correct weight and fibre for the fabric. Choose a sewing machine needle appropriate for the type of thread and fabric.

STRESS POINTS

Reinforce areas that will be under strain with a second line of stitching just inside the first ie. underarms, crotch, elbows.

Friendship, AS&E 57

FLAT SEAM

A flat seam is the most common method used to join two pieces of fabric together and is suitable for most fabrics. The two fabrics are positioned with right sides together and raw edges matching. A line of straight machine stitching is worked at a consistent distance from the raw edges. The seam can then be trimmed and the raw edges neatened together or separately.

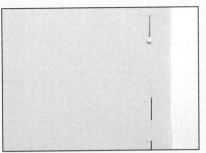

1. Matching raw edges, place the fabric right sides together. Pin.

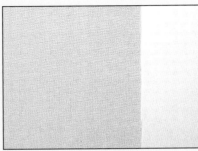

2. Machine stitch the seam. Press.

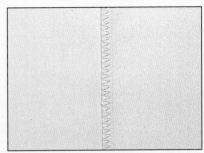

3. Trim and neaten as required. Press again from the right side.

FLAT FELLED SEAM

This type of reinforced seam is particularly suited to children's overalls where extra strength is needed. When finished with topstitching, it can be decorative as well as practical. This seam requires an allowance of 1.5cm (5/8").

1. Matching raw edges, place the fabric right sides together. Pin and stitch 1.5cm (5/8") from the raw edge.

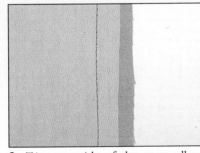

2. Trim one side of the seam allowance to 1cm (3/8").

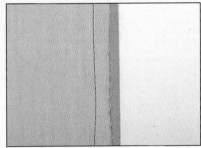

3. Fold over the 5mm (3/16") extension from the second side of the seam allowance, enclosing the trimmed side. Press.

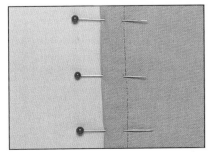

4. Open out the fabric and press the seam to one side. Pin in place.

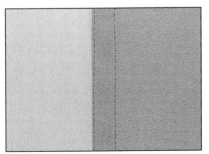

5. Work a line of topstitching close to the folded edge.

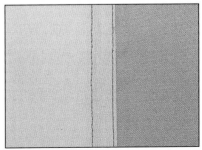

6. If desired, turn to the right side and work a second line of topstitching close to the seam.

FRENCH SEAM

The Dream Catcher, AS&E 37

French (double) seams create a beautiful finish on the inside of the garment as the seam is sewn twice, fully enclosing the raw edges. They are particularly suited to translucent and sheer fabrics where the seams may show through.

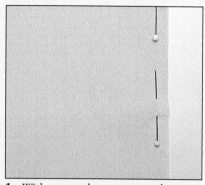

1. With raw edges even and wrong sides together, pin the two pieces of fabric.

2. Using a straight machine stitch, stitch within the seam allowance 5mm (³/₁₆") from the stitchline.

3. Trim the seam allowance to 2 - 3mm (¹/₈"), ensuring that the edge is straight and even.

4. Press the seam flat. With right sides together, fold with the stitchline exactly along the fold. Press again and pin together.

5. Stitch along the stitchline. The raw edges from the previous seam are enclosed within the stitching.

6. Press the seam flat and to one side. Press again from the right side.

HINT

After working the first line of stitching, press and spray starch the seam before trimming. This will help prevent it from fraying and causing 'whiskers' after the second line of stitching is complete.

BOUND SEAM

Out of Africa, AS&E 43

Bound (Hong Kong) seams are a luxurious finish for coats and jackets. The raw edge of each side of the seam allowance is fully enclosed with a bias strip. Cut bias strips 2.5cm (1") wide.

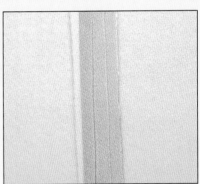

1. Stitch a flat seam and press the seam allowance open.

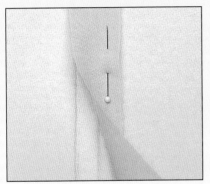

2. With right sides together and matching raw edges, pin a bias strip along the length of one seam allowance.

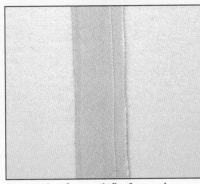

3. Stitch, 6mm (¼") from the raw edge.

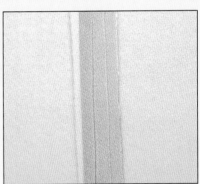

4. Fold under 6mm (¼") on the remaining long edge of the binding.

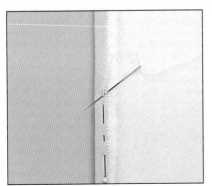

5. Fold the binding around the edge of the seam allowance and hand or machine stitch in place.

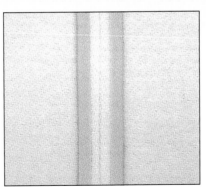

6. Repeat for the remaining seam allowance.

HINT

Press the actual stitches of a seam to flatten them and 'meld' them into the fabric before pressing the seam in the required direction or into the required shape.

TURNING THROUGH SEAMS

When turning through, care must be taken to ensure that the fabric is turned through completely. This is particularly important with collars and cuffs. A point turner and seam creaser is specifically designed for this. Angled points can be particularly difficult and as these have the fabric trimmed close to the seam on the inside, care must be taken to ensure that the raw edge is not pushed through the seam to the outside. Reducing the stitch length at the points or stitching a second row as reinforcing will help prevent this from happening.

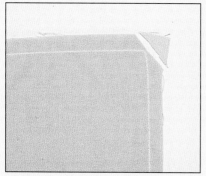

1. Stitch the seam. Trim and clip where necessary.

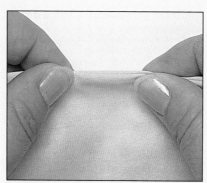

2. Turn the fabric to the right side. Roll the fabric between your fingers to bring the seam to the edge.

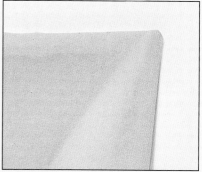

3. Push the point turner up into the point, forcing the fabric to the outside.

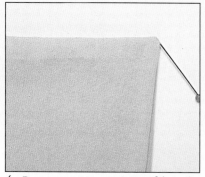

4. Remove any remaining fabric by inserting a pin into the point and pushing the fabric out. Do not pull the fabric from the outside as you may pull the raw edge through the seam.

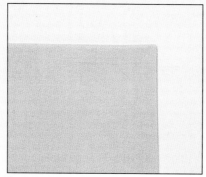

5. Press.

CLIPPING AND TRIMMING

Most seams benefit from being trimmed, reducing the seam bulk and eliminating unsightly bulges once the seam is pressed.

Piccolini, AS&E 37

GRADING SEAMS

A graded seam has each layer trimmed to a different width, reducing the overall bulk. This is particularly suited to seams where there are thick fabrics or more than two layers of fabric eg. neckline seam.

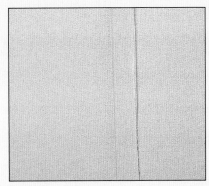

1. Stitch the seam.

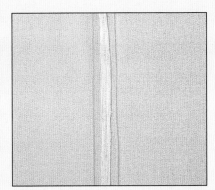

2. Trim each layer by a successively greater amount.

CONCAVE CURVES

Curved seams must be clipped to enable the fabric to be turned smoothly to the right side. The more acute the curve, the closer the clipping needs to be.

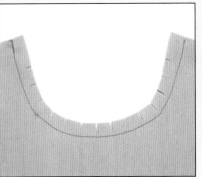

1. Trim the seam allowance and clip with single cuts down to the stitching line.

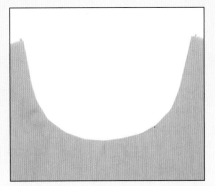

2. Turn to the right side. The cuts will enable the seam allowance to fan out.

CONVEX CURVES

Ensure that all of the fabric is pushed out of the seam before pressing. A point turner or thick knitting needle is handy for doing this.

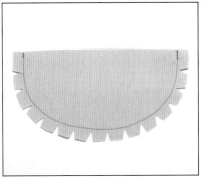

1. Trim the seam allowance and clip by removing V-shaped sections along the length of the seam.

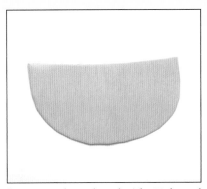

2. Turn to the right side. The V-shaped cuts will enable the the seam allowance to close up and fit into the reduced space.

UNDERSTITCHING

Understitching helps to prevent an inner part of a garment
(eg. facing or lining) from rolling to the outside.

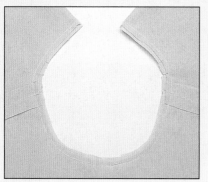

1. Stitch the seam. Trim the seam allowances and clip any curves. Press the seam away from the garment.

2. Keeping the outer part of the garment out of the way, stitch on the right side of the facing or lining close to the seamline through all layers.

Moonshadow, AS&E 42

TOPSTITCHING

Topstitching creates a decorative finish as well as reinforcing a seam.
Special topstitching thread creates a better finish than normal machine sewing thread as it is a heavier weight.
Use a longer stitch length than for normal stitching.

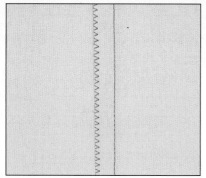

1. Stitch the seam. Trim the seam, neaten and press towards the side to be topstitched. Press again from the right side.

2. Stitch an even distance away from the seam along its length.

HINT

Topstitching can be worked in thread that contrasts, rather than blends with the fabric. This can be particularly effective, but take care with your stitching as any errors will be more noticeable.

CONSTRUCTION

ASSEMBLING THE GARMENT

While there are a multitude of variations you can use to make your garment unique, the basic method required to assemble a smocked dress is the same.

Child of the Universe, AS&E 37

Country Garland, AS&E 44

Unforgettable, AS&E 44

Puppy Love, AS&E 39

Bellisima, AS&E 38

Child's Play, AS&E 46

Rosebud, AS&E 57

Babycakes, AS&E 64

ORDER OF WORK - SQUARE YOKE DRESS

1. STITCH THE SHOULDER SEAMS

1. With right sides together and aligning the stitchlines, pin the front and back together at the shoulders.

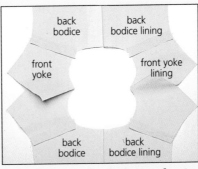

2. Stitch. Repeat for the linings, forming a circle. Press the seams open.

3. With wrong sides together, place the front yoke over the yoke lining and refold the back bodices and linings.

2. FINISH THE NECKLINE OR ATTACH THE COLLAR See pages 65 - 73 and 96 - 102.

3. ATTACH THE FRONT SKIRT WITH PIPING - METHOD 1

Piping is a perfect finishing touch and also serves to reinforce the seam between the smocked panel and the yoke.
By stitching the piping to the skirt first, it is possible to have it perfectly positioned in relation to the smocking.
An alternative method uses double sided tape to position and hold the piping until the yoke is attached.
Backsmock the stitchline or holding row to hold the pleats upright when the piping and yoke are stitched in place.

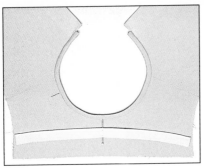

1. Cut a length of piping to fit the front yoke. Mark the centre front.

2. Matching centres, pin and tack the piping to the smocked panel, positioning it an even distance from the top row of smocking.

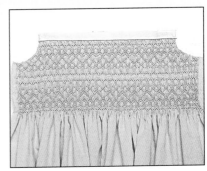

3. Stitch in place just inside the piping stitchline.

ATTACH THE FRONT SKIRT WITH PIPING - METHOD 1... CONTINUED

4. With right sides together and matching centre fronts, pin and tack the yoke to the piped skirt with the previous stitchline uppermost.

5. Stitch, carefully following the previous stitchline.

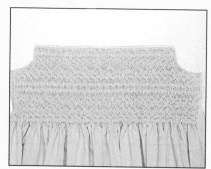

6. Grade the seam to reduce the bulk.

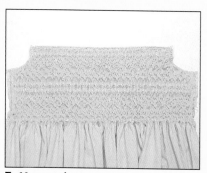

7. Neaten the seam.

8. Press under 1cm (⅜") on the lower edge of the yoke lining.

9. Pin in place, enclosing the seamline.

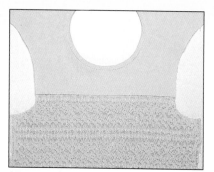

10. Hand stitch in place along the previous stitchline. Press.

11. Completed yoke attached to the front skirt with piping.

Sherbert Fizz, AS&E 59

ATTACH THE FRONT SKIRT WITH PIPING - METHOD 2

The yoke can also be attached to the smocked panel from the right side using a piped lapped seam, also known as 'stitching in the ditch'. This method involves piping the lower edge of the yoke and pressing under the seam allowance. The yoke is then positioned over the smocked skirt and the two pieces are joined by stitching in the space between the piping cord and the previous stitchline. This is particularly suited to shaped yokes.

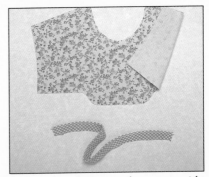

1. Fuse interfacing to the wrong side of the yoke. Cut a piece of piping to fit the shaped lower edge of the yoke.

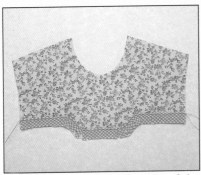

2. Pin piping to the right side of the yoke, clipping to fit the curves where necessary. Stitch, following the piping stitchline.

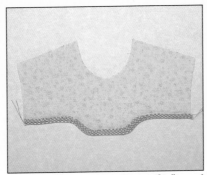

3. Trim the seam to 5mm (3/16") and press to the wrong side.

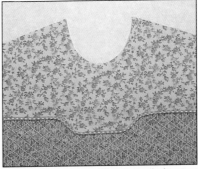

4. Matching centre fronts and aligning the piping on the straight edges with the first row of smocking, position the yoke over the smocking. Pin and tack in place.

5. Attach the yoke to the skirt, stitching in the ditch between the piping and the yoke.

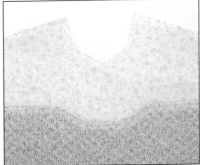

6. Trim away the smocked panel in the shaped area behind the yoke. Neaten the raw edges.

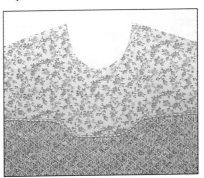

7. Press, taking care not to crush the smocking.

4. PIPE THE BACK BODICE

Piping reinforces the seam between the back bodice and the skirt and makes a neat finish.

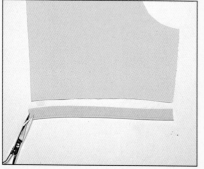

1. Cut two lengths of piping, each the width of the back bodice plus a 1cm (³⁄₈") extension. Remove the cording from the extension.

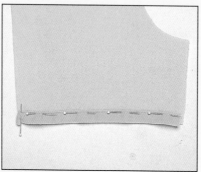

2. Open out the back bodice and lining. Pin the piping in place along the stitchline, curving the extension into the seam allowance.

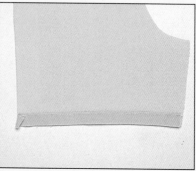

3. Stitch in place along the piping stitchline. When attaching the back skirt, stitch from the bodice side, between the corded edge of the piping and the previous stitchline.

5. MAKE THE PLACKET See pages 103 - 106.

6. GATHER THE BACK SKIRT

Once the placket has been constructed the back skirt fullness must be controlled before it is attached to the back bodice pieces. This can be done by gathering or pleating.

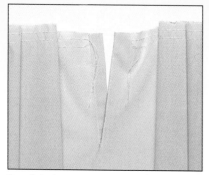

1. Stitch two rows of machine gathering across the top edge of each side of the back skirt, excluding the placket.

2. Pull up the threads to match the back bodices.

Water Baby, AS&E 63

7. ATTACH THE BACK SKIRT - METHOD 1

Once the back skirt has been prepared it is attached to the back bodice and lining. The bodice lining can be attached in two ways.

1. With right sides together and matching raw edges and centre back foldlines to placket edges, pin the skirt to the back bodice.

2. Stitch, ensuring the lining is out of the way. Remove the gathering threads. Trim and neaten the seam.

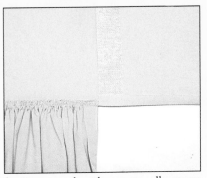

3. Press under the seam allowance on the bodice lining.

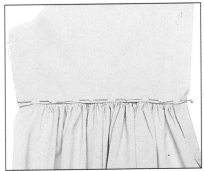

4. Pin in place aligning the folded edge with the previous stitchline.

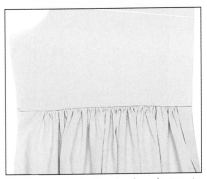

5. Hand stitch the bodice lining in place. Press.

TRACING PATTERNS

If you have a favourite pattern, trace it onto a lightweight cardboard. When cutting out the garment, draw around this cardboard pattern, remove the pattern and then cut out. This avoids any accidental nicks in the pattern and you pattern stays perfect forever.

Spring Bouquet, AS&E 60

7. ATTACH THE BACK SKIRT - METHOD 2

1. Follow steps 1 and 2 in method 1. Trim and neaten the seam.

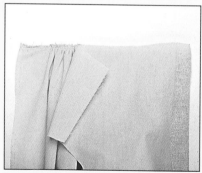

2. Fold the lining around the skirt, sandwiching the skirt between the bodice and the lining.

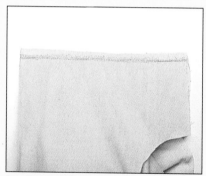

3. Pin and stitch, following the previous stitchline.

4. Trim the seam. Turn to the right side and press.

5. Completed back bodice attached to skirt.

GATHERING FABRIC

Use three rows of machine stitching instead of the traditional two rows. Place one row on the stitching line and then another row 5mm (3/16") either side of this one. Use a stitch length of 2.5 and do not loosen the tension. This means that you create a lot of pretty little gathers rather than large loose gathers. Pull up all three bobbin threads together to the desired measurement. After stitching, remove the gathering threads. Sometimes with Christening gowns and little girl's dresses, there is a lot of fabric to be gathered into a small space and this method ensures that the gathers sit flat and are much easier to handle. The small stitches also make it easier to keep the gathered piece to the desired length and not lose the gathers at the ends.

Winter Garden, AS&E 59

Bear Hug, AS&E 46

8. MAKE AND ATTACH THE SASHES OR BELT

See pages 107 - 114.

9. STITCH THE SIDE SEAMS

Side seams can be stitched with flat or French (double) seams.
Avoid French seams on very thick fabrics as the resulting seam will
be very bulky and unsightly.
Catching the end pleat on the smocking into
the seam will ensure that the smocking thread ends are more secure.

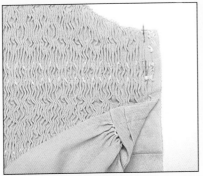

1. With right sides together and matching raw edges, begin pinning the side seams at the base of the back bodice. Align the lowest row of smocking with the back bodice seam.

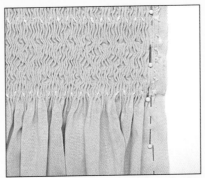

2. Continue pinning up towards the armhole and down towards the hem.

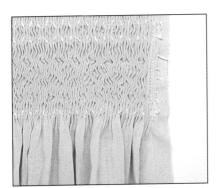

3. Beginning at the armhole, stitch the seam.

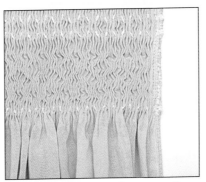

4. Trim and neaten the seam. Press towards the back. Repeat for the second side seam.

10. ADD SLEEVES OR FINISH THE ARMHOLES

See pages 60 - 62 and 115 - 124.

Flowers of Africa, AS&E 45

11. WORK THE BUTTONHOLES AND ATTACH THE BUTTONS

See pages 74 - 82.

Princess Priya, AS&E 55

12. FINISH THE HEM

See pages 83 - 91.

ORDER OF WORK - FULL BODICE DRESS

1. STITCH THE SHOULDER SEAMS

 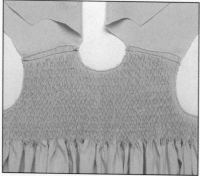 

1. Block and shape the smocked bodice following the instructions on pages 25 or 26.

2. With right sides together and aligning stitchlines, pin and stitch the front to the two back bodice pieces at the shoulders. Press the seams to the back.

3. Attach the front bodice lining to the two back bodice lining pieces at the shoulders to form a circle. Press the seams open. With wrong sides together, fold the lining to the inside.

2. FINISH THE NECKLINE OR ATTACH THE COLLAR See pages 65 - 73 and 96 - 102.

3. PIPE THE BACK BODICE (OPTIONAL) See page 54.

4. MAKE THE PLACKET See pages 103 - 106.

5. GATHER THE BACK SKIRT See page 54.

6. ATTACH THE BACK SKIRT See pages 55 - 56.

7. MAKE AND ATTACH THE SASHES OR BELT (OPTIONAL) See pages 107 - 114.

8. STITCH THE SIDE SEAMS See page 57.

9. ADD SLEEVES OR FINISH THE ARMHOLES See pages 60 - 62 and 115 - 124.

10. WORK THE BUTTONHOLES AND ATTACH THE BUTTONS See pages 74 - 82.

11. FINISH THE HEM See pages 83 - 91.

ORDER OF WORK - BISHOP DRESS

The front, back and sleeves are stitched together before the pleating and smocking are worked.

1. FINISH THE BUTTON BAND OR PLACKET See pages 63 - 64 and 103 - 106.

2. FINISH THE NECKLINE See pages 96 - 102.

3. STITCH THE SLEEVE AND SIDE SEAM

 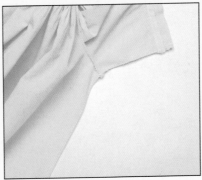 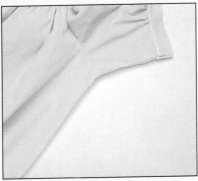

1. With right sides together and matching raw edges and seams, pin the underarm and side seam.

2. Stitch. Trim and neaten the seam.

3. Press towards the back. Press again from the right side.

Liberty Rose, AS&E 65

4. FINISH THE LOWER SLEEVE EDGES

See pages 115 - 124.

5. WORK THE BUTTONHOLES AND ATTACH THE BUTTONS

See pages 74 - 82.

6. FINISH THE HEM

See pages 83 - 91.

Morgan, AS&E 56

ARMHOLES

If sleeves are not a part of your garment, the armhole will require finishing. Bindings and variations on bindings, are the most popular to use.

Paper Dolls, AS&E 52

Coquette, AS&E 59

Riverdance, AS&E 49

Mimi, AS&E 56

Star of the Show, AS&E 48

Little Sweethearts, AS&E 38

Tiger Lily, AS&E 57

Sunshine, AS&E 60

BINDING THE ARMHOLE EDGE

Do not trim or neaten the armhole seam before binding. Cut a bias strip of fabric 2.5cm (1") wide and long enough to go around the armhole plus 2cm (3/4"). Fold in 5mm (3/16") on one long raw edge and press.

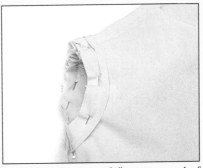

1. Fold under 1cm (3/8") at one end of the strip. Beginning at the underarm with the folded end, pin the raw edge of the strip around the armhole, overlapping the folded end.

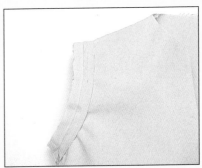

2. Stitch 1cm (3/8") from the raw edge.

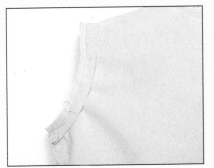

3. Trim the seam to 5mm (3/16").

4. Fold the strip to enclose the seam. Handstitch in place along the previous stitchline.

HINT

To ensure a smooth finish, always use binding strips that are cut on the bias. Stretch them ever so slightly as you apply them.

BINDING THE LOWER ARMHOLE ON A BISHOP GARMENT

Cut a bias strip 4cm (1 1/2") longer than the distance between the finished sleeve edges.

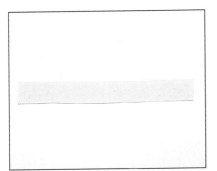

1. Fold the strip in half along the length and press.

2. With right sides together and matching raw edges, pin the strip to the armhole. Overlap the sleeve on both sides. Fold back raw ends. Stitch.

3. Fold the binding to the wrong side enclosing the seam allowance. Hand stitch in place along the previous stitchline.

PIPED AND BOUND ARMHOLE

If using a pattern not specifically designed for bound armholes, cut away the seam allowance on the armhole.
You may find that cutting more away at the upper part of the armhole gives a better finish.
Cut a length of piping and binding to fit around each armhole plus 2cm (3/4") for seam allowances.
Remove 1cm (3/8") of piping cord from each end of the piping.

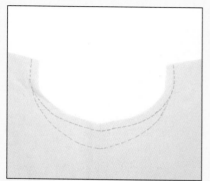

1. Trim the armhole as desired.

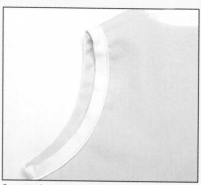

2. With right sides together and matching raw edges, pin and stitch the piping around the armhole, curving into the seam at the underarm.

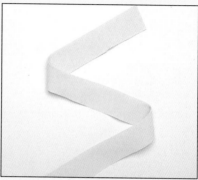

3. Fold each binding strip in half along the length and press.

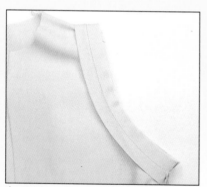

4. Fold under 1cm (3/8") at one end of the binding strip. Beginning with the folded end at the underarm, pin the binding to the armhole. Overlap the ends by 1cm (3/8") and trim away any excess. Stitch, following the previous stitchline.

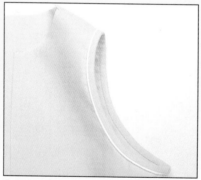

5. Trim the seam. Fold the binding to the wrong side enclosing the seam allowance. Hand stitch in place.

Party Time, AS&E 63

HINT	When using piping, first trim the heading so it is the same width as the seam allowance. Align the raw edges of the heading with the raw edges of the garment.

BUTTON BANDS

As well as being functional, button bands can become a decorative feature of your garment. They can be plain, piped, edged with lace, embellished with embroidery and the showcase for beautiful buttons.

Colonial Girl, AS&E 35

Tiny Treasure, AS&E 61

Woven Dreams, AS&E 31

Ming Blue, AS&E 64

Miss Daisy, AS&E 58

The Little Shepherd, AS&E 62

Chérie, AS&E 44

Anna, AS&E 65

DETACHED BUTTON BAND

Whether a button band is attached to the front or the back of a garment,
it is worked in the same way.

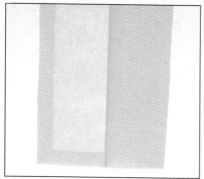

1. With wrong sides together, fold the button band in half along the length and press. Unfold and fuse interfacing to the wrong side of one half.

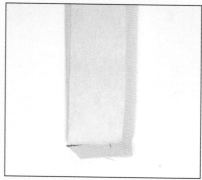

2. Refold the button band with right sides together. Stitch across the lower end 1cm (3/8") from the raw edge. Clip the corner and press.

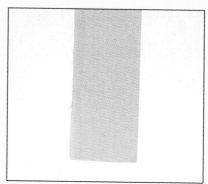

3. Turn through to the right side and press.

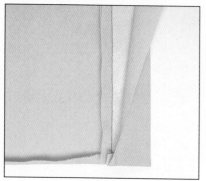

4. Fold the skirt hem and press. With right sides together, pin and stitch the button band to the garment keeping the facing free.

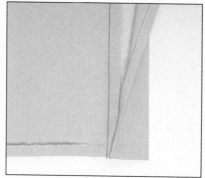

5. Press the seam towards the band. Fold under the seam allowance on the facing and press.

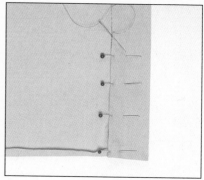

6. Hand stitch the facing to the wrong side of the garment along the previous stitchline.

PERFECT CORNERS

To achieve a perfect corner, mark the fabric at the point where the two stitchlines would intersect. Stop stitching just before reaching this point. Turn the wheel on your machine by hand until the needle is exactly at the mark. With the needle in the fabric, lift the presser foot and turn the fabric. Lower the presser foot and continue stitching along the second stitchline.

COLLARS

A piped Peter Pan collar is the classic finish for a smocked yoke dress but many other collar shapes can be used. Ideally the collar should not obscure the smocking or sit over the head of the sleeve. The collar should sit together at both the centre front and centre back.

Sea Maiden, AS&E 40

Field of Dreams, AS&E 52

Moppet's Day Out, AS&E 51

Australian Wildflowers, AS&E 32

Goodness, AS&E 45

Mikah, AS&E 63

Little Sweethearts, AS&E 59

Les Marguerites, AS&E 41

BINDING A COLLAR

To prepare the binding, fold the strip in half along the length and press. If the collar pattern is not specifically designed with a bound edge, it is necessary to trim away the outer edge seam allowance to ensure a correct fit. Do not trim the neck edge on the collar.

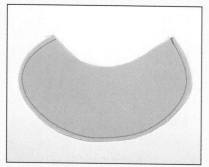

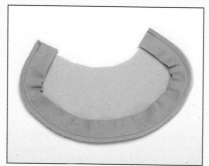

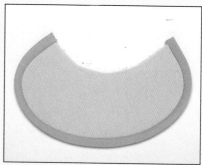

1. With wrong sides together, baste the collar pieces together just inside the stitching line.

2. With right sides together and matching raw edges, pin and stitch the binding around the outer collar edge.

3. Fold the binding, enclosing the seam allowance. Trim the seam allowance if necessary. Hand stitch in place along the previous stitchline. Press.

WORKING WITH COLLARS

If using a collar on a baby garment, catch the under collar to the front yoke to prevent the collar from flipping onto the baby's face.

The collar should roll off the neckline in a gentle curve. To enable it to do this, the collar neckline curve must be more open than the garment neckline curve.

True Colours, AS&E 43

Before applying the collar, roll the undercollar up so that 2 - 3mm (1/8") extends at the neck edge.

Pin and tack the collar and under collar together along the neck edge.

This helps the collar roll nicely off the neckline and pulls the outer seam of the collar under so that the under collar does not show.

PIPED PETER PAN COLLAR

Texas Rose, AS&E 52

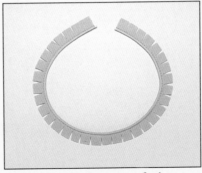

1. Cut a length of piping to fit the outer edge of the collar. Clip the piping heading at 6mm (¹/₄") intervals or as necessary.

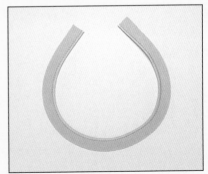

2. Alternatively, press a length of piping to follow a curve.

3. Matching the piping stitchline to the collar stitchline, pin the piping to the outer edge of the right side of each collar. Tack in place.

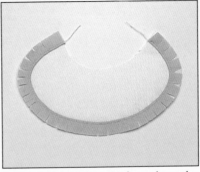

4. Stitch the piping in place along the piping stitchline. Remove the tacking.

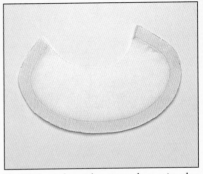

5. With right sides together pin the under collar in place. Stitch between the corded edge of the piping and the previous stitchline.

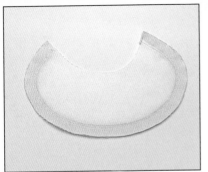

6. Stitch again 2-3mm (¹/₈") away, within the seam allowance.

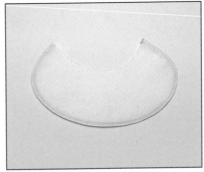

7. Trim very close to the second row of stitching.

8. Turn to the right side. Finger press by rolling the piping between your fingers and smoothing out the curves. Press.

FRILLED COLLAR

There are a number of ways to finish a collar with a frill. Frills can be single or double layered and cut on the bias or straight grain. We have chosen a method that tapers the frill into the collar at the centre front and back. This method eliminates the need to adjust the collar pattern.

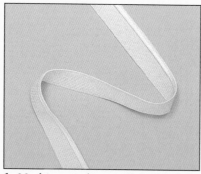

1. Machine stitch a small double hem along one long edge of each frill strip.

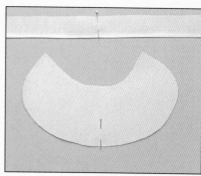

2. Divide the strip and collar into two by placing a pin at the halfway point.

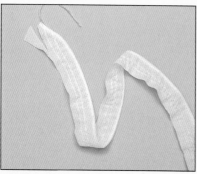

3. Work two rows of machine gathering 6mm (¼") apart, tapering at each end with the first row 7mm (5/16") from the raw edge. Trim away excess fabric from the end.

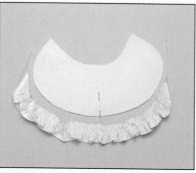

4. Pull up the gathering threads until the strip is approximately the same length as the outer edge of the collar.

5. Matching pins and with right sides together, pin the frill to the collar. Ensure the edge of the frill runs into the seam allowance 1cm (⅜") down from the neck edge of the collar. Adjust the gathers evenly.

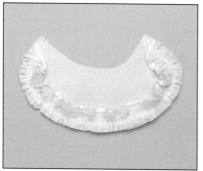

6. Stitch the frill in place along the stitchline. Remove the pins.

7. Pin the frilled collar piece to the under collar, sandwiching the frill between the two layers.

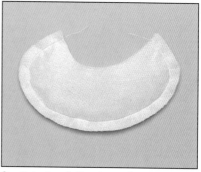

8. Stitch, following the previous stitchline. Remove the gathering threads.

FRILLED COLLAR... CONTINUED

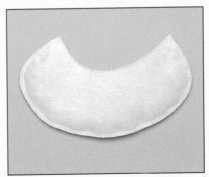

9. Stitch again 2-3mm (⅛") away within the seam allowance.

10. Trim close to the second line of stitching.

11. Turn through to the right side and press carefully. Finished frilled collar.

PIPED AND FRILLED COLLAR

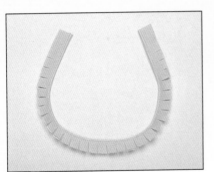

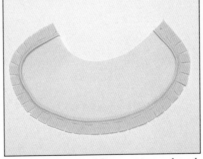

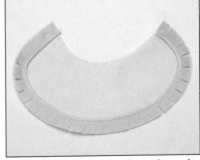

1. Cut a length of piping to fit the outer edge of the collar. Clip the piping heading at 6mm (¼") intervals or as necessary.

2. Matching stitchlines, pin and tack the piping to the outer edge of the right side of the collar.

3. Stitch the piping in place along the piping stitchline.

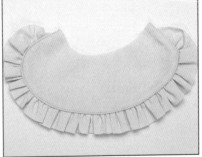

Fireside Friends, AS&E 50

4. Prepare the frill following steps 3-4 on page 68. Pin the frill onto the piped collar aligning the frill stitchline with the previous stitchline. Baste.

5. Continue constructing the collar following steps 6-11 on pages 68-69.

EMBROIDERED COLLAR

An embroidered collar adds a delightful finishing touch to a smocked garment. Working the embroidery before the collar pieces are cut out will prevent unwanted stretching of the bias cut neck edge of the collar. It enables the embroidery to be worked in a hoop if desired. Transfer the collar shaping and embroidery design with lead pencil if using fusible interfacing.

1. Transfer the collar shapes and embroidery designs onto the fabric taking care to align the grainlines.

2. Fuse or tack interfacing to the back of the fabric rectangle.

3. Work the embroidery designs.

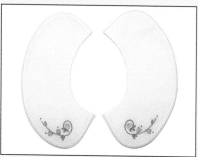

4. Cut out the collar along the marked cutting lines. Construct the collar.

HINT

Spray the fabric with starch and press before transferring the design. The starch will form a barrier between the fabric and the pencil and any marks will wash away easily.

EMBROIDERING A COLLAR AFTER CONSTRUCTION

Some embroidery is best done after the collar is constructed, particularly designs that follow the collar shaping. Interface the upper collar pieces. This helps to prevent show through if carrying threads.

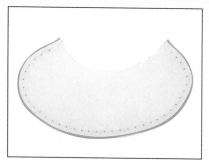

1. Stitch the collar pieces together. Trim the seam to 2-3mm (⅛"). Turn to the right side and press. Mark the embroidery design onto the fabric.

2. Separate the collar layers at the neck edge.

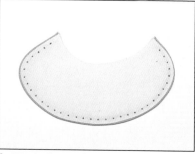

3. Work the embroidery through the neckline opening, taking care not to catch the under collar.

COLLAR WITH FAGGOTING

Faggoting, or twisted insertion stitch, can be used to join fabrics together or as in this case, a rouleau strip to the edge of a collar. This creates an open, lacy look.

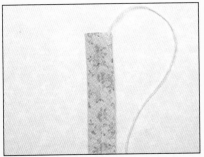

1. Cut bias strip to required width. With right sides together and matching raw edges, pin and stitch strip. Begin at the raw edge and taper in to form a funnel. Leave long tails on threads.

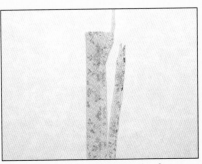

2. Stitch again just beside the first row of stitching. Trim the seam allowance to 3mm (⅛").

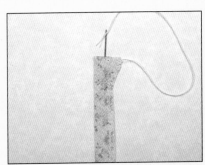

3. Knot the tails onto a tapestry needle. Take the needle down through the tube.

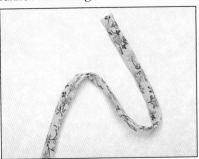

4. Ease the needle through the tube and pull the strip through to the right side. Press with the seam along one edge.

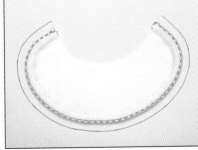

5. Tack the piped collar to a piece of stiff paper. Draw a line around the collar, 5mm (³/₁₆") away from the piped edge.

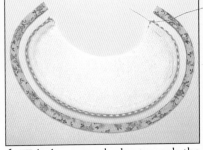

6. With the seamed edge towards the piping, press the rouleau to fit the marked curve. Tack the rouleau to the paper.

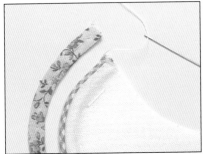

7. Secure the thread on the outer edge of the collar.

8. Pick up 2 - 3 threads through all layers of the rouleau. Ensure that the loop of thread is behind the needle.

9. Pull thread through. With the thread behind the needle, pick up 2-3 piping fabric threads approx 2 - 3mm (⅛") away from the secured thread.

COLLAR WITH FAGGOTING... CONTINUED

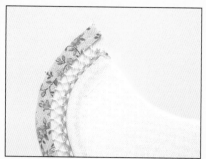

10. Pull the thread through. Take a stitch as before through the rouleau 2 - 3mm (¹/₈") away from the first stitch.

11. Continue working around collar, alternating stitches. On sharper curves, the distance between the stitches on the piped edge is gradually reduced.

12. Remove the collar from the paper by carefully clipping the tacking stitches.

ATTACHING THE COLLAR

A beautifully applied collar is one of the most important elements of a well constructed garment. The collar pieces should meet at both the front and the back of the neckline and the collar should roll off the neckline in a soft curve.

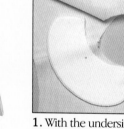

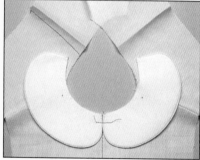

1. With the underside of the collar to the right side of the yoke and keeping the linings out of the way, pin the collar pieces to the neckline at the centre front.

2. Tack the collar fronts together at the stitchline.

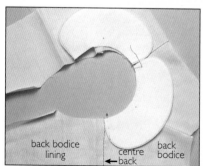

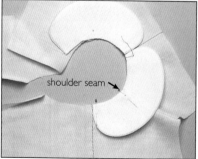

3. Pin the back edge of one collar piece to the back bodice at the centre back point.

4. Match the shoulder mark on the collar to the shoulder seam. Pin.

5. Pin the remaining sections of the collar to the neckline.

ATTACHING THE COLLAR... CONTINUED

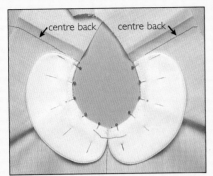

6. Repeat for the remaining collar piece.

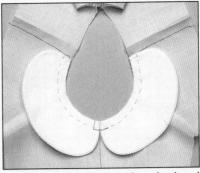

7. Baste the collar in place by hand or machine.

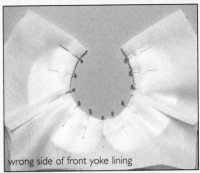

8. With right sides together and matching raw edges and shoulder seams, fold the yoke lining over the yoke. Pin in place around the neckline.

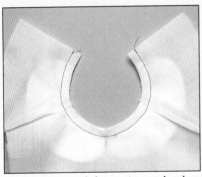

9. Stitch around the entire neck edge, reinforcing the stitching at each end.

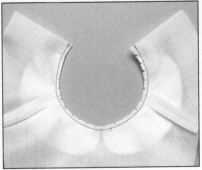

10. Grade the seam, clip the corners and curves.

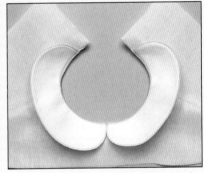

11. Turn the yoke and collar to the right side.

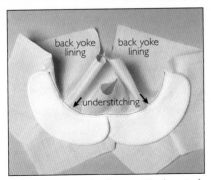

12. Open out the lining. Understitch the seam allowance to the lining, 2 - 3mm ($^1/_8$") from the seam.

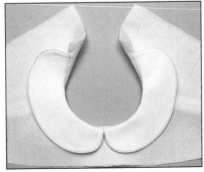

13. Turn the lining to the inside. Gently press the neck edge.

FASTENERS

Fasteners are used to secure the openings that allow the garment to be put on and taken off easily. The most commonly used fastener on smocked garments is the button but snap fasteners, hooks and eyes, zips and popper studs are also used.

Primrose, AS&E 30

River of Diamonds, AS&E 45

Summer Dreams, AS&E 61

First Blush, AS&E 44

Gypsy, AS&E 62

Jemima, AS&E 38

Elektra, AS&E 33

Solitude, AS&E 54

BUTTONS

Buttons are available in an infinite number of sizes, styles, shapes and colours. It is simply a matter of choosing the one that is right for the garment.

Buttons are available in flat or shank styles. A flat button has two or four holes through the surface to enable it to be secured to the garment. A shank button has an extension on the back through which the button is secured. Avoid using shank buttons on the back of baby garments as the extension will press into the child's back when lying down.

Do not make the buttons on baby garments too small. Remember that adult fingers have to undo and do them up. Stitch buttons on with a strong thread. The thread may match or contrast with the button. If the button does not come with a shank, a thread shank can be made when attaching it to the garment. The purpose of a shank is to hold the button away from the surface of the fabric. When buttoned up, the thickness of the buttonhole will sit comfortably beneath the button without causing the fabric to pucker.

Shisha, AS&E 43

Home Coming, AS&E 66

Sugar Plum Fairy, AS&E 51

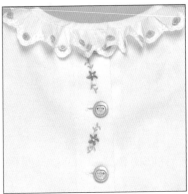

Celebrations, AS&E 43

ATTACHING A BUTTON WITH A BULLION BUD

Bullion buds are a decorative way of attaching buttons. A four-hole button gives you more scope to be creative but a delicate rosebud can be worked on a two-hole button.

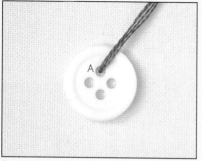

1. Secure the thread on the back. Position the button on the fabric so the holes form a diamond. Bring the thread to the front through the upper hole (A).

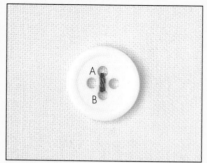

2. Take the thread to the back of the fabric through the lower hole (B). Pull the thread firmly to anchor the button.

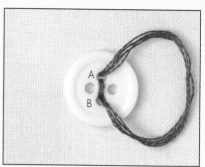

3. Emerge at A. Take needle to the back at B. Pull the thread through, leaving a large loop of thread on the front.

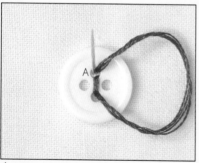

4. Re-emerge at A and leave the needle in the button. Hold the needle firmly on the back of the fabric.

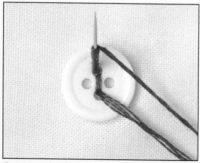

5. Wrap the loop of thread around the needle in a clockwise direction for the required number of wraps. Ensure they are evenly packed together.

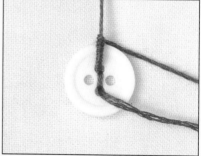

6. Holding the wraps securely, carefully pull the thread through.

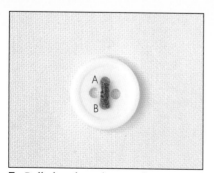

7. Pull the thread towards you until the wraps are even and lie firmly against the button. Take the thread to the back at B and end off.

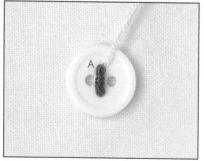

8. Change thread colour. Secure the thread on the back and emerge at A, just to the right of the inner petal.

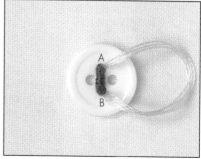

9. Take the needle to the back at B, just to the right of the inner petal. Pull the thread through leaving a large loop on the front as before.

ATTACHING A BUTTON WITH A BULLION BUD... CONTINUED

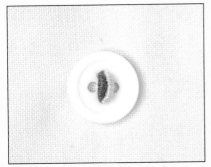

10. Work the bullion knot in the same manner as before. Ensure it lies to the right of the inner petal.

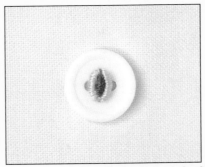

11. Stitch a bullion knot on the left of the inner petal in the same manner to complete the bud.

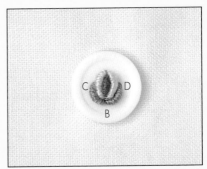

12. Change thread colour. Work bullion knots from C to B and from D to B for leaves. End off the thread.

ATTACHING A BUTTON WITH AN EMBROIDERED FLOWER

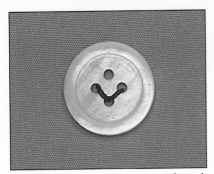

1. Using matching sewing thread, attach the button with the holes positioned to form a diamond.

2. Work a stitch from A to B using green embroidery thread.

3. Work a second stitch from C to B to form the leaf on one side.

4. Work another stitch from D to B to form the second leaf. End off the thread securely on the back.

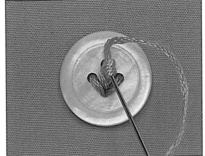

5. Work a large French knot at A, taking care not to pull the knot through the hole.

6. End off the thread securely on the back.

MAKING A THREAD SHANK

Ideally, the shank should be roughly the same length as the thickness of the button band. The thicker the fabric, the longer the shank needs to be. Using a shank prevents unsightly puckering. The spacer used to create a gap for the shank, in this instance a match, can be placed above or below the button.

HINT

The length of a buttonhole should be the diameter plus the thickness of the button used.

The length of the thread shank should be the thickness of the garment at the buttonhole plus 3mm ($1/8$") for movement.

Strawberry Thieves, AS&E 41

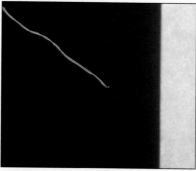

1. Mark the positions for the buttons on the fabric. Secure the thread at one marked position.

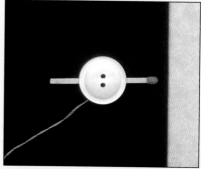

2. Place a match (or similar object) at the button mark on the fabric. Centre the button over the match at the marked position.

3. Stitch the button in place finishing with the thread on the back.

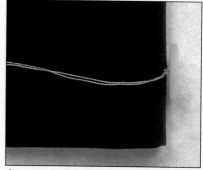

4. Bring the thread to the front between the button and the fabric, close to the stitching. Gently pull out the spacer.

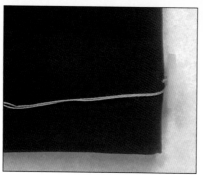

5. Wrap the thread around the stitching five or six times to create the shank.

6. Take the thread to the back and end off.

HANDMADE BUTTONHOLES

Buttonholes that are made by hand add an extra special touch. They are particularly suited to delicate fabrics but can be worked on most garments. Mark the buttonhole on the fabric and cut the opening.

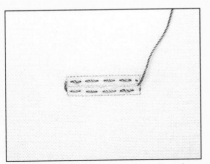

1. Beginning at the right hand end on the upper half of the buttonhole, work running stitch as indicated. Bring the thread to the surface through the opening.

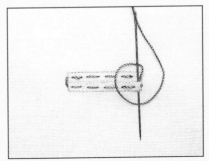

2. Take the needle through the opening and emerge on the lower line. Wrap the thread anti-clockwise behind the eye and then the tip of the needle.

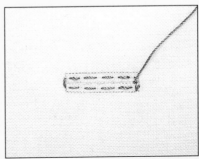

3. Pull the thread through, pulling towards you then upwards towards the opening.

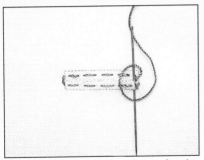

4. Take the needle through the opening and emerge next to the previous stitch. Wrap the thread around the needle as before.

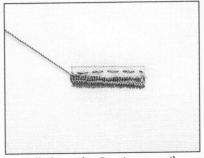

5. Pull through. Continue until you reach the end of the opening. Keep the stitches as close as possible.

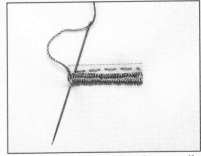

6. First bartack. Take the needle through the opening and emerge next to the previous stitch. Do not wrap the thread around the needle.

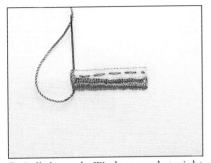

7. Pull through. Work several straight stitches across the end. Take the needle to the back at the upper edge, next to the last stitch.

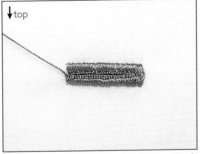

8. Turn the fabric upside down. Work buttonhole stitch across the second side.

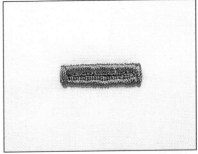

9. Make a bartack as in step 7. Take the needle to the back, weave throught the stitching and trim.

THREAD LOOP

When the back of a dress is fastened correctly, a small flap of the back bodice or yoke will extend beyond the button at the neckline. This occurs on garments with or without collars, or with bound necklines. Even if the flap is under a collar, fastening this extension helps the neckline to sit correctly at the back. A tiny button and thread loop or hook and eye are perfect finishing touches.

Saltbush, AS&E 31

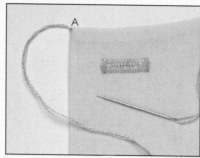

1. Using a long doubled thread, bring the needle out at the top of the folded edge (A). Take one or two tiny back stitches to secure the thread.

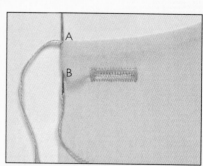

2. Take the needle from B to A between the two layers of fabric. The distance between A and B is approx the width of the button.

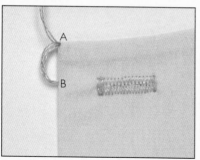

3. Pull the needle through. Take the needle from B to A again, forming a four thread loop.

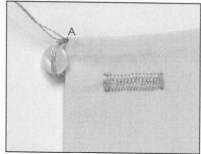

4. Test for size by slipping the button through the loop. Adjust if necessary. Secure the thread at A with tiny back stitches.

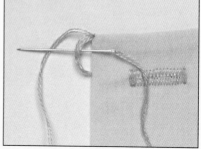

5. To work the blanket stitch, take the needle under the loop and over the thread.

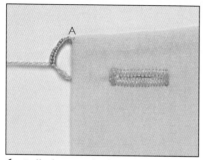

6. Pull the stitch firmly towards A. Continue stitching over the loop, packing the stitches firmly together.

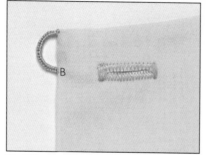

7. When the loop is covered by blanket stitches, secure the thread at B. End off the thread.

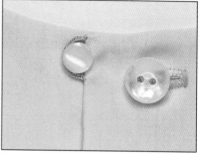

8. Attach the button to correspond with the loop.

PLACING AND ATTACHING BUTTONHOLES AND BUTTONS

To ensure that the garment closes correctly, the buttons and buttonholes must be placed so the centre back pieces are aligned when the garment is buttoned. The same principle applies to front buttoning garments.
In general, lap the right back over the left for girls garments and vice versa for boys.
Our example shows the back bodice of a girl's garment.

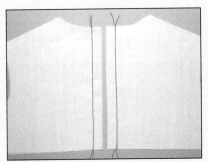

1. Refer to your pattern piece to locate the placement of the centre back. Mark with pins, tack or baste if you wish.

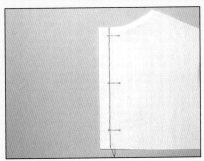

2. Mark the placement for the buttonholes by tacking or with a water-soluble marker.

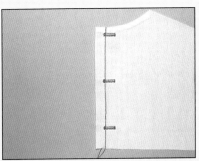

3. Stitch the buttonholes, beginning at the end closest to the edge of the back bodice.

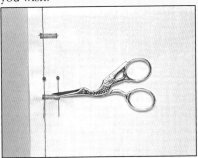

4. Using a seam ripper or small sharp scissors, cut open each button-hole. Place a pin at each end of the buttonhole to prevent cutting too far.

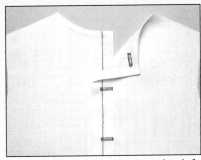

5. Lap the right back over the left, aligning the centre backs.

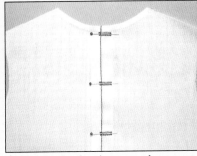

6. To mark the button placement, place a pin through the end of the buttonhole, at the centre back marking.

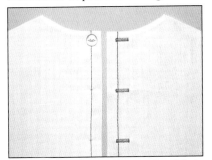

7. Mark the pin position with a fabric marker. Attach the buttons at the marked points.

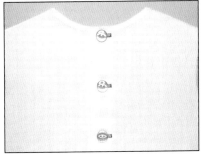

8. Completed buttons and button-holes.

The Tea Party, AS&E 48

OTHER FASTENERS

Self-cover Buttons

Self-cover buttons can be made to coordinate perfectly with the fabric of a dress. It is also possible to embroider onto the fabric before making the button.

Carefully follow the manufacturer's instructions. Buttons can also be covered commercially.

Periwinkle, AS&E 30

HINT

When making self-cover buttons, add a dab of craft glue to the well of the button cover before gathering the fabric onto it. Pull the fabric around the shape and push it into the glue. This holds the fabric firmly when securing the back of the button.

Hook and Eye

A hook and eye or hook and thread loop can be used at the neck of a garment to secure the top of the back opening. These metal fasteners are available in many sizes and several colours.

Popper Studs

Popper studs are particularly useful for crotch openings on rompers and overalls. They are easy to apply and come in a range of colours and finishes. They are also suitable for other openings. Follow the manufacturer's instructions.

Bundles of Joy, AS&E 34

Snap Fasteners

Snap fasteners are often used on bishop garments where it is not possible to make a buttonhole through the smocked fabric. They are designed to be invisible and are available in metal or plastic finishes. Choose a colour that matches the fabric.

Blue Heeler, AS&E 32

Zips

Although not often used on smocked garments, zips are suited to some fabrics and styles. If using a zip, it is unnecessary for the back bodices to overlap one another. Cut the back bodice and lining pieces separately with the cut edge 1cm (3/8") out from the centre back. Omit the placket from the back skirt. The back skirt will require a centre seam.

HEMS

A hem forms a finish on the lower edge of the skirt. It can be plain or decorated with tucks, embroidery or lace insertions. As well as finishing the lower edge, the hem also serves to weight the skirt, helping it to hang nicely. A generous hem enables the skirt to be let down as the child grows taller. The lower edge of the skirt can also be bound or finished with a frill.

Earth Angel, AS&E 46

Sugar Plum Fairy, AS&E 51

Versailles, AS&E 34

Country Cousins, AS&E 36

Gloria, AS&E 50

Teardrops, AS&E 32

PLAIN HEM

When using this technique, the stitching should be almost invisible from the right side.
Best results are achieved when you do not pull the stitches firmly.

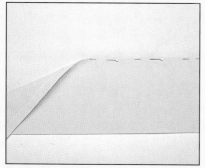

1. Turn under 1cm (⅜") on the entire hem edge and press. Turn under a further 9cm (3½") and pin in place. Press.

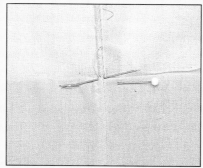

2. Beginning at one side seam, secure the thread on the wrong side of the fabric.

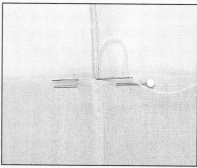

3. Slide the needle through the hem fold for 6mm - 1cm (¼" - ⅜").

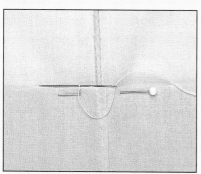

4. Pick up one or two threads of the skirt fabric as close to the hem fold as possible.

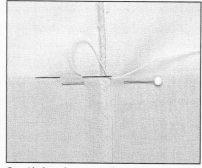

5. Slide the needle through the hem fold for another 6mm - 1cm (¼" - ⅜"). Pick up one or two threads of the skirt fabric.

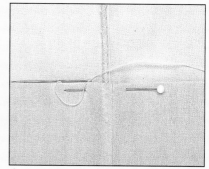

6. Continue in this manner around the hem. Press.

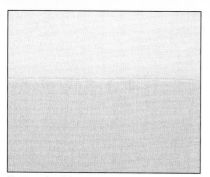

7. Finished hem.

8. Finished hem from the front.

Irish Eyes, AS&E 42

FALSE HEM

Once a skirt has been let down to its full extent a false hem or hem facing is needed to finish the lower edge and maintain the hang of the skirt. If matching fabric is unavailable choose a similar coloured fabric that is the same weight and with the same fibre content. Pre-wash to eliminate any shrinkage. Wide hemming tape is also suitable and is commercially available.

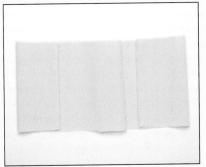

1. Cut two strips 12cm (4 ¾") deep by the required width plus seam allowances. Stitch the strips together forming a circle.

2. Fold under 1cm (⅜") on one raw edge and press.

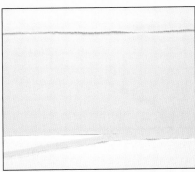

3. With right sides together and matching raw edges and side seams, pin the circle to the skirt. Stitch. Trim the seam to 5mm (³⁄₁₆"). Press.

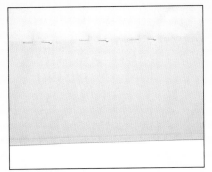

4. Fold the strip to the inside of the skirt with the seam 6mm (¼") up from the folded edge. Press and pin in place.

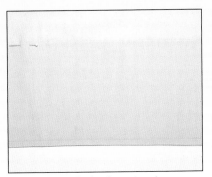

5. Hand stitch the hem in place.

HINT

As an alternative, use a contrast fabric. Stitch the right side of the band to the wrong side of the skirt then turn the band to the outside. Finish by hand or machine. This can also be done with a shaped upper edge.

Marzipan, AS&E 29

SCALLOPED HEM

Scallops can be used to finish the lower edge of a garment. This edge would also be very pretty on a sleeve or neckline. Varying the size of the scallops will result in different effects.

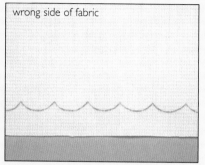

1. Carefully trace the scallop shaping onto the wrong side of the fabric.

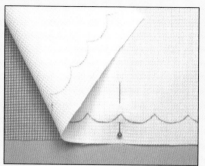

2. With right sides together, pin the lining to the skirt.

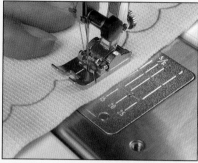

3. Using a short, straight stitch, begin stitching along the marked line. Stitch very slowly and follow the line exactly.

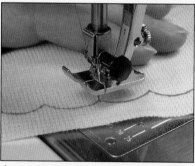

4. At the scallop peaks, stop with the needle down in the fabric. Raise the presser foot and pivot the fabric.

5. Lower the presser foot and continue the stitching as precisely as possible.

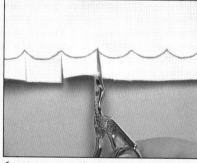

6. Using small sharp scissors, clip almost to the stitching at the scallop peaks.

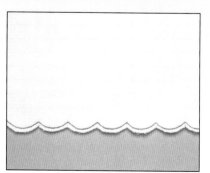

7. Trim the seam allowance to 2 - 3mm (⅛").

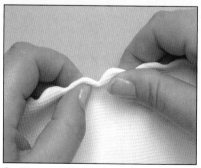

8. Turn to the right side. Roll each scallop between thumb and forefinger to ease the scallop into shape.

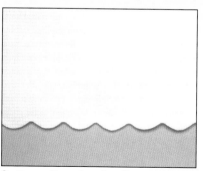

9. Press. Completed scallops.

HEM TUCKS

These are sometimes called growth tucks as they are easy to release as the child grows.

Tucks add interest to the hem of the skirt but must be positioned carefully to achieve the correct balance.

Tucks can vary in number and width and hemming into a tuck is a quick way of finishing the lower edge. If adding tucks to a skirt, allow twice the finished tuck depth eg. a 2.5cm (1") tuck requires an extra 5cm (2") of skirt depth. Add the required amount for tucks before cutting out.

Little Leprechaun, AS&E 48

HEM TUCKS

1. Measure up from the raw edge to the point at which the tuck is to be stitched.

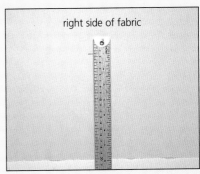

2. Measure down the depth of the tuck and mark with a fabric marker.

3. Measure from the raw edge to the mark.

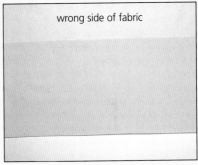

4. Working from the wrong side, turn up and pin this amount around the entire hem edge. Remove the fabric marker. Press.

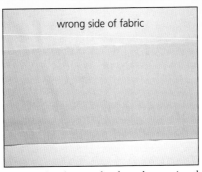

5. Stitch the tuck the determined width from the folded edge.

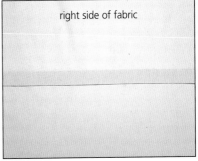

6. Unfold the fabric and press the tuck towards the hemline.

HEMMING WITH A TWIN NEEDLE TUCK

This technique is particularly effective on sheer or translucent fabrics such as voile, organza or batiste. It is suited to scalloped and other curved or angled designs as the fabric will not pull away from the stitching.

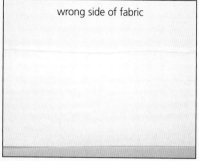

1. Fold up the hem, press and tack in place.

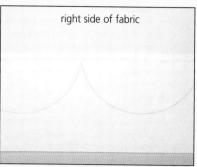

2. Mark the upper hem shaping onto the right side of the skirt with a water-soluble marker.

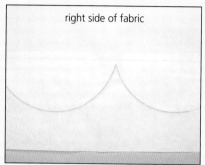

3. Using the twin needle, stitch along the marked line through both layers.

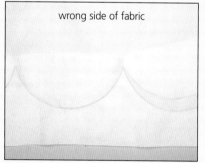

4. Remove the tacking. On the wrong side, carefully cut away the excess fabric.

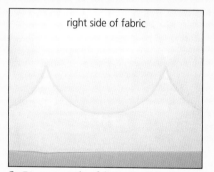

5. Rinse out the fabric marker. Press.

HINT

Avoid using this technique with loosely woven fabric or with straight lines of stitching as the fabic will fray and pull away.

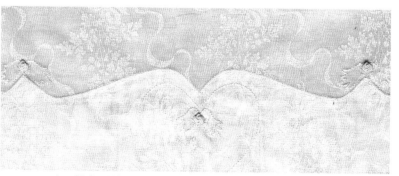

Angel Baby, AS&E 40

HEMMING INTO A TUCK

By using this method, you not only make a pretty hemline tuck, but the hem is invisibly and quickly secured at the same time. Our sample shows a portion of the hem and a single hemline tuck.

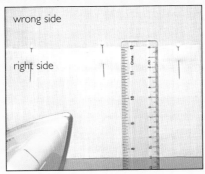

1. Fold under the hem for the required depth. Pin in place. Press the fold.

HINT

When working pintucks, only mark the position of the first pintuck. Use the grooves in the pintuck foot as a spacing guide for further tucks.

wrong side

right side

2. Using long machine stitches, baste close to the raw edge.

wrong side

previous fold

new fold

3. Fold again to form a double hem. The raw edge is aligned with the new fold. Press.

Giggles, AS&E 58

right side

4. With the right side facing and the hem underneath, stitch around the skirt at the required distance from the lower fold. The raw edge is enclosed within the tuck.

right side

tuck

5. Remove the basting and press the tuck and hem downwards.

Homeward Bound, AS&E 36

BOUND EDGE

The lower edge of the skirt can be finished with a binding of matching or contrasting fabric. If the lower edge is straight the binding can be cut on the straight grain or the bias. If the lower edge is shaped, the binding should be cut on the bias. Purchased bias binding is ideal for this task. Press open one folded edge before you begin.

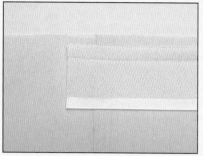

1. With right sides together, matching stitchlines and beginning at one side seam, pin the unfolded edge of the binding to the hemline. Allow 1cm (3/8") to extend pass the seam.

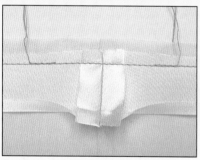

3. With right sides facing, stitch the binding ends together using a 1cm (3/8") seam. Press the seam open. Stitch the remainder of the binding to the hemline.

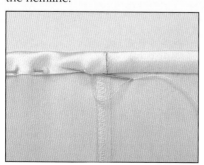

5. Hand stitch the fold of the binding to the previous stitchline.

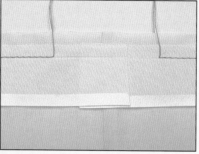

2. Overlap the ends of the binding allowing 1cm (3/8") to extend past the seam. Trim any excess binding. Stitch, beginning and ending approximately 3cm (1 1/8") from the seam.

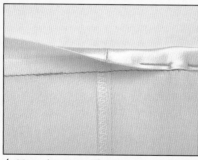

4. Trim the seam if necessary. Fold the binding over to the wrong side, enclosing the raw edges, and pin with folded edge aligned with stitching.

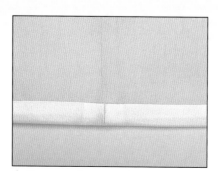

6. Press gently.

LAYERED SKIRTS

When the skirt has two or more different layers of fabric, each can be finished separately either to the same or different lengths.

Silver Lining, AS&E 32

Heaven Blessed, AS&E 60

STRAIGHTENING THE LOWER EDGE OF A BISHOP

Depending on the pattern used, a bishop neckline may cause the hemline to droop at the centre front and back.
To correct this, the lower edge will require straightening before the hem is stitched.
You will need a long ruler and a fabric marker suitable for the fabric.

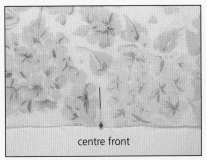

1. Find the centre front and mark with a pin at the lower edge.

2. Hang the garment on a coat hanger and mark the shoulder line with pins.

3. Remove the coat hanger. Lay the garment flat, folded at the shoulders. Keeping side seams straight and centre front mark visible, evenly fold the fullness of the skirt.

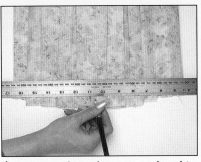

4. Position the ruler across the skirt with one edge level with the lower edge of the side seams. Mark the centre front with the fabric marker.

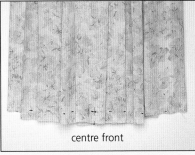

5. Lightly mark several more points around the skirt. Remove the ruler.

6. Open out one half of the front skirt. Rule a line between the marked points.

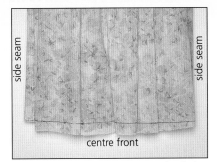

7. Repeat for the other half of the front skirt.

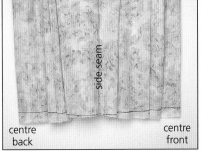

8. Using the centre back seam as the midpoint, repeat steps 3 - 7 on the back skirt. The lines will meet at the side seams.

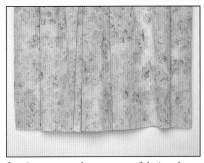

9. Cut away the excess fabric along the marked lines.

INSERTS

Inserts can be a beautiful addition to a smocked garment. They allow you to create a garment with reduced fullness.

Bonnie Lass, AS&E 44

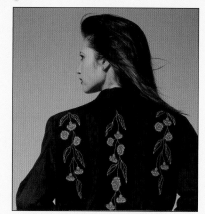

Australian Nights, AS&E 25

Bright Sparks, AS&E 62

Joshua, AS&E 56

The Perfumed Garden, AS&E 47

Ruffled Feathers, AS&E 39

Happy Holiday, AS&E 64

Farmyard Friends, AS&E 40

INSERTS

Inserts can be added as a patch or can run across the entire width of the garment.

1. Cut a piece of lining fabric the same size as the smocked insert. With wrong sides together, pin and tack the lining to the insert.

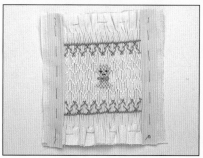

2. Cut a length of piping to fit each side. Pin and tack the side pieces very close to the first and last pleats.

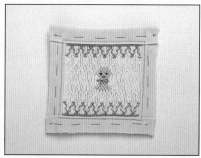

3. Pin and tack the remaining pieces to the upper and lower edges. Machine stitch around all sides along the piping stitchline. Trim any excess fabric level with the piping.

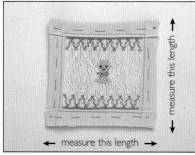

4. Carefully measure the rectangle formed by the piping stitchline.

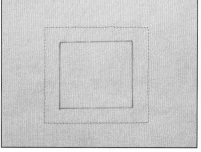

5. Using a fabric marker, rule a rectangle to these measurements on the garment. Rule a second rectangle 1cm (3/8") inside the first. Staystitch around the outer rectangle.

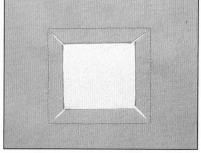

6. Cut out the inner rectangle and clip into the corners of the outer rectangle.

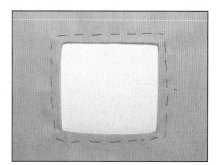

7. Turn the seam allowance to the wrong side, concealing the staystitching. Tack in place approximately 6mm (1/4") from the folded edges.

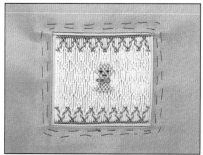

8. Centre the insert under the opening. Pin and tack the insert in place as close as possible to the edges.

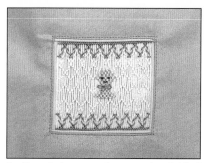

9. Topstitch very close to the folded edges. Remove the tacking. Trim and neaten the seams.

INTERFACINGS

Interfacings can be fusible or non-fusible, woven or non-woven,
and come in a range of weights.

INTERFACING THE BUTTON BANDS

The button and buttonhole areas on a square yoke garment are subject to considerable stress and
should be reinforced to prevent the button tearing away from the fabric and the buttonhole distorting.

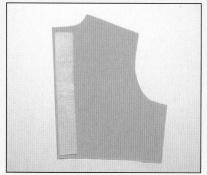 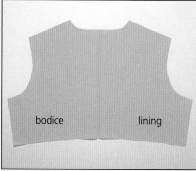 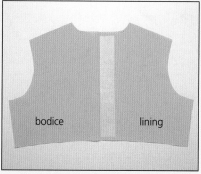

1. Cut a strip of interfacing to the required size. Press the back bodice along the foldline.

2. Open out the back bodice and lining. Place onto the ironing board with the wrong side uppermost.

3. Position the interfacing on the lining with the glue side down and one long edge along the foldline. Press, fusing the interfacing in place.

INTERFACING THE COLLAR AND SLEEVE BANDS

If using non fusible interfacing, do not remove seam allowances.
Tack layers together just beyond the seam allowance.

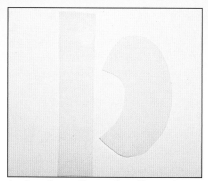 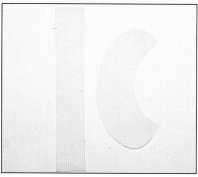 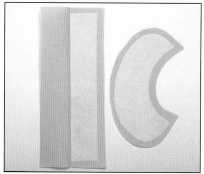

1. Cut the collar and cuff interfacing to the required shape.

2. Trim the seam allowance away on the interfacing pieces.

3. Position the interfacing on the wrong side of the cuff lining and the collar. Fuse in place.

LININGS

Garments can incorporate linings that cover the back of the smocking (known as full linings) or linings that finish at the seam directly above the smocking. This type of lining is attached to the garment around all sides. A full lining extends to the base of the smocking but is not attached at the lower edge. The edge of the lining can be finished with a small hem or a decorative machine stitch such as a scallop. A full lining can be used on full bodice or basic square yoke garments. The lining conceals the back of the smocking and prevents the smocked fabric from stretching excessively.

USING A FULL LINING

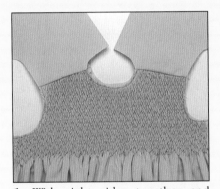

1. With right sides together and aligning stitchlines, pin and stitch the front to the back bodice pieces at the shoulders. Repeat for the linings to form a circle. Press the seams. Fold the lining into position and press.

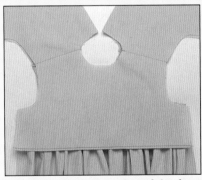

2. Neaten the lower edge of the front bodice lining or finish with a narrow hem.

3. Attach the back skirt to the back bodice and lining following the instructions on pages 55 and 56.

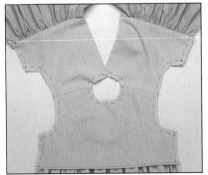

4. With wrong sides together, pin and tack the lining around the neckline, armholes and along the side.

5. The two layers will now be treated as one.

HINTS

Silk is weakened by perspiration and so it does not make a good lining fabric. A silk garment is best lined with an alternative fabric.

NECKLINES

Necklines can be finished in a variety of ways and can be as plain or as fancy as you wish. As well as attaching a collar they can be piped, bound, embroidered, frilled, shaped or any combination of these.

Snow White, AS&E 28

Calypso, AS&E 49

Bella, AS&E 54

Harlequin, AS&E 51

Celebrations, AS&E 43

Gidget, AS&E 62

Tea with Isabella, AS&E 50

The Birthday Girl, AS&E 40

When using a pattern not specifically designed with bound edges it is necessary to trim away the garment seam allowance before attaching the binding to ensure a correct fit. A binding should be an even width along its length. After stitching the binding in place, take care not to trim away too much of the seam allowance. Enough should remain to fill the binding, making it firm and smooth. Refer to pages 22 and 23 for information on how to determine the width of bias strips and the positioning of the stitchline.

BINDING A BASIC SQUARE YOKE NECKLINE - METHOD 1

To prepare the neckline, fold the lining to the inside and press along the back bodice foldlines. Tack the yoke, bodice and lining together just inside the stitchline. To prepare the binding, fold the strip in half lengthwise and press. Mark the centre of the strip and the centre front of the neckline.

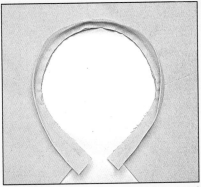

1. With right sides together and matching centre fronts, pin and stitch the binding around the neck edge with 1cm (⅜") extending at both ends.

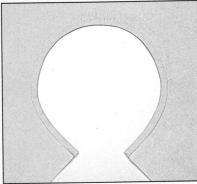

2. Fold in the ends of the binding. Fold the binding, enclosing the seam allowance. Pin and hand stitch in place along the previous stitchline. Press.

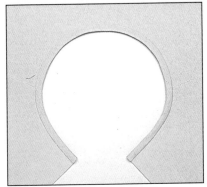

3. Completed neckline binding.

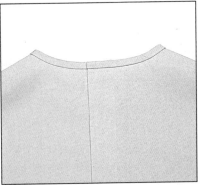

4. Finished neckline with binding overlap.

HINT

Cut bindings on the true bias. The most accurate way to find this is to pull a thread on both the lengthwise and crosswise grain of the fabric and fold the fabric to match the pulled thread lines.

Honey 'N Spice, AS&E 42

BINDING A BASIC SQUARE YOKE NECKLINE - METHOD 2

This method can also be applied to a bishop with a button band.
To prepare the binding, fold the strip in half along the length and press.

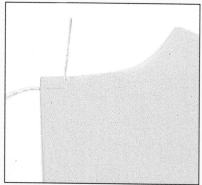

1. With right sides together, fold each back bodice and lining along the centre back foldline. Beginning on the neck edge at the marked centre back, stitch down 6mm (¼"). Pivot and stitch across to the folded edge.

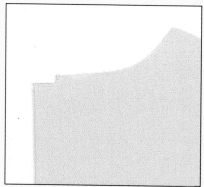

2. Clip into the corner. Trim the seam. Turn to the right side and press. Tack the two layers together at the neck edge. Repeat for the remaining back bodice.

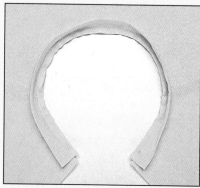

3. With 1cm (⅜") extending at both ends, pin and stitch the binding around the neck edge.

4. Fold in the ends of the binding. Fold the binding enclosing the seam allowance, pin and hand stitch in place along the previous stitchline. Press.

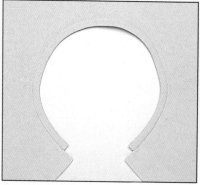

5. Completed neckline binding.

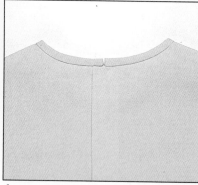

6. By eliminating the overlap of the neckline binding the bulk at the neckline is reduced and a flatter finish is achieved. This is particularly suited to necklines finished with lace or fabric frills.

| HAND STITCHING THE BINDING | When hand stitching, stitch with the bias. If you make each stitch straight the binding will pucker. Begin at the centre front and turn the garment as you stitch. Return to the centre front and hand stitch the second half. |

BINDING A BISHOP NECKLINE

The neckline binding should be smooth and even in width along its entire length. The binding can be applied with or without piping. To prepare the binding, fold the strip in half lengthwise and press. Mark the centre of the strip and the centre front of the neckline.

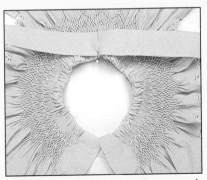

1. With right sides together, match and pin the centre of the binding to the centre front.

2. With 1cm (⅜") extending at each end, pin the binding at the back fold on each side.

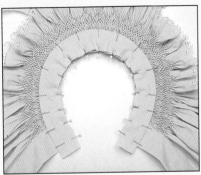

3. Carefully adjust the pleats to ensure that they are even. Pin the binding at the armhole seams. Pin the remainder of the binding in place.

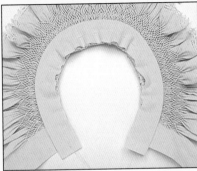

4. Tack the binding to the neckline along the stitchline ensuring that the stitchline is an even distance from the smocking.

HINT

Backsmock the stitchline with stem or outline stitch. This will hold the pleats upright and prevent them from being flattened when the binding is stitched in place. The line of stitching will also make it easier to keep the binding an even distance from the top row of smocking when pinning and tacking it in place.

5. Stitch the binding in place. Trim the seam. Fold in the ends then fold the binding to the back enclosing the seam allowance. Pin and hand stitch in place along previous stitchline. Press.

6. Completed neckline binding.

Curlylocks, AS&E 53

PIPING THE NECKLINE

Piping gives a neat, crisp finish to the neckline edge. It is particularly suited to garments for small babies, where a collar would flip onto the child's face when lying down. The piping can match or contrast with the garment.

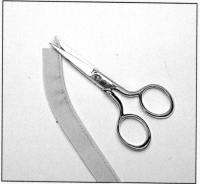

1. Cut a length of piping to fit the neckline allowing a 1cm (⅜") extension at each end. Remove the cord from the extensions.

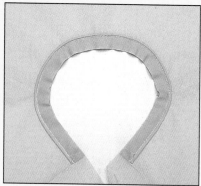

2. Pin and tack the piping to the neckline, curving the extension into the seam allowance. Stitch. Remove the tacking.

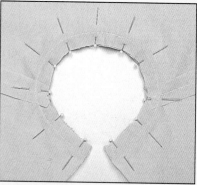

3. With the previous stitchline uppermost, fold the linings over the back bodices and front yoke. Pin in place.

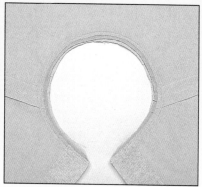

4. Stitch, following the previous stitchline. Grade and clip the seam allowance and corner.

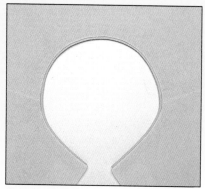

5. Turn to the right side and press.

Petite Flower, AS&E 63

STITCHING PIPING TO SMOCKED FABRIC

Loosen the foot pressure by half when stitching piping to smocked fabric. This helps to prevent the pleats from being pushed to one side.

PIPING AND BINDING THE NECKLINE

When using a pattern not specifically designed for bound edges, trim away the seam allowance before attaching the binding. This ensures a correct fit. To prepare the binding, fold the strip in half along the length and press. Cut a piece of piping the same length as the binding strip. Trim the piping heading to 6mm (1/4").

HINT

Take care when handling bias strips as they can be easily stretched out of shape. Once this happens, they cannot be returned to their original size.

Flora, AS&E 61

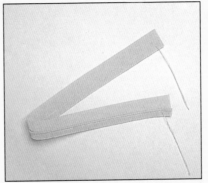

1. With right sides together and matching raw edges, tack then stitch the piping and binding together leaving 1cm (3/8") unstitched at both ends. Remove the cord from each end of the piping extension.

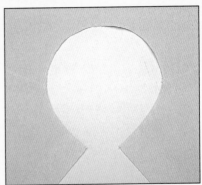

2. Tack the yoke, bodice and lining together around the neckline just beyond the stitchline.

3. With 1cm (3/8") extending at both ends, pin and stitch the binding around the neckline, following the previous stitchline and sandwiching the piping between.

4. Fold in the ends of the piping and the binding. Fold to the back enclosing the seam allowance and hand stich in place along the previous stitchline. Press.

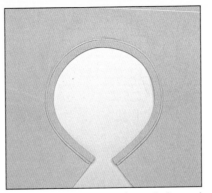

5. Completed piped and bound neckline.

FABRIC AND LACE FRILLS WITH BINDING

A fabric or lace frill creates a soft neckline finish. A fabric frill can be made from the same or contrasting fabric. Lace is available in a variety of widths and finishes.

Choose a lace with similar fibre content and care requirements as the garment fabric. To prepare the binding, fold the strip in half along the length and press.

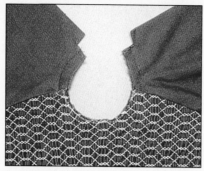

1. Prepare the neckline following steps 1 and 2 on page 98.

2. Mark the centre of the lace. Make a small hem at each end of the lace strip and hand stitch in place. Work a row of gathering along the lace heading. Alternatively pull a gimp thread in the lace heading.

Fifi, AS&E 35

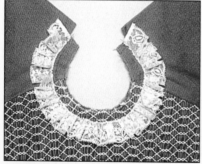

3. Matching centres and centre backs and with the right side uppermost, pin the lace to the neckline with the base of the heading just above the stitchline. Check that the gathers are evenly distributed. Tack in place.

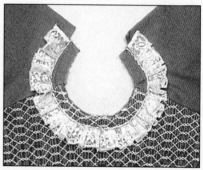

4. Stitch the lace in place. Remove the tacking.

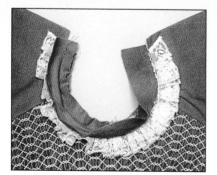

5. With right sides together, raw edges even and matching centres, pin the binding to the neckline. Stitch in place following the previous stitchline.

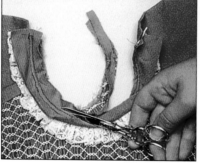

6. Stitch the entire neck seam on the stitchline. Stitch again, 4mm (³/16") from previous stitching. Trim very close to the second row of stitching.

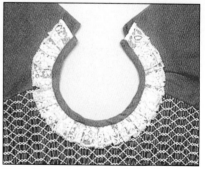

7. Fold in the ends of the binding. Fold the binding, enclosing the seam allowance. Hand stitch in place along the previous stitchline. Press.

PLACKETS

Plackets are openings that allow for ease of dressing. They are most commonly used in back skirts and at the lower edges of sleeves.

Sugar Mouse, AS&E 34

Bambini, AS&E 35

Sea Sprite, AS&E 59

Golden Feece, AS&E 32

Duet, AS&E 44

Raggedy Anne, AS&E 36

The Littlest Milkmaid, AS&E 33

Rhapsody, AS&E 28

MAKING THE CENTRE BACK PLACKET - UNSEAMED FABRIC

1. Crease a fold for a short distance down the centre of the back skirt. Mark the fold with a line the required distance from the upper edge.

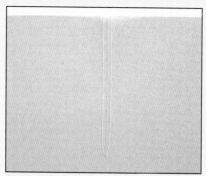

2. Staystitch along both sides of the line, beginning 2 - 3mm (1/8") away at the upper edge and tapering to a point at the lower end.

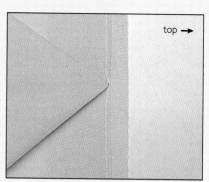

3. Cut down the line, taking care not to cut the stitching at the point. Spread the cut edges. With right sides together, position the staystitching just above the placket stitchline.

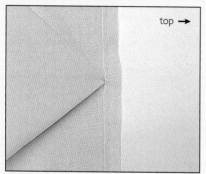

4. Pin and stitch, taking care not to form a pleat at the centre.

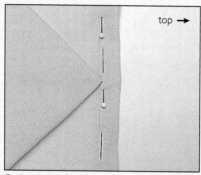

5. Press under the seam allowance on the remaining long edge of the placket. Fold the placket over the seam allowance to the wrong side and pin in place.

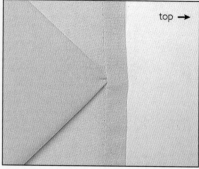

6. Hand stitch the folded edge to the previous stitchline.

7. Stitch a diagonal line at the folded base of the placket.

8. Press the right side of the placket under and leave the left side extended.

Evangeline, AS&E 50

MAKING THE CENTRE BACK PLACKET - SEAMED FABRIC

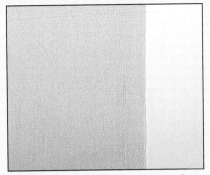

1. Stitch the centre back seam from the marked point to the hemline.

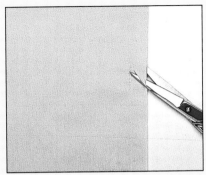

2. Clip the seam allowance, angling the cut up to the end of the stitching.

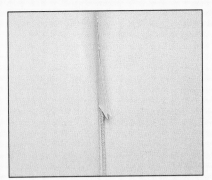

3. Trim and neaten the seam below the clipped point. Press the seam to one side.

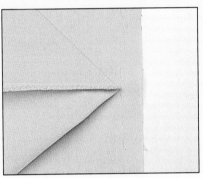

4. Pin and tack the placket strip along both sides of the opening.

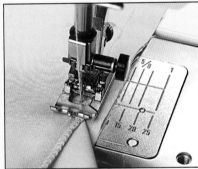

5. With the skirt uppermost, stitch down one side of the opening, folding the excess fabric out of the way and ensuring that the first stitch of the centre back seam is caught in the stitching.

6. With the needle in the fabric, raise the presser foot and move the excess fabric out of the way. Lower the presser foot.

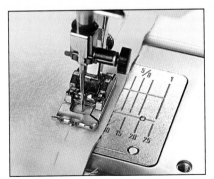

7. Continue stitching along the second side.

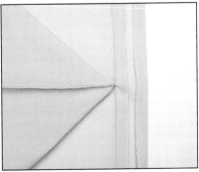

8. Press the seam towards the placket. Press under the seam allowance on the remaining long side of the placket strip.

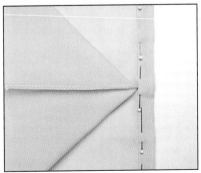

9. Fold the pressed edge over the seam allowance to the wrong side and pin in place.

MAKING THE CENTRE BACK PLACKET - SEAMED FABRIC... CONTINUED

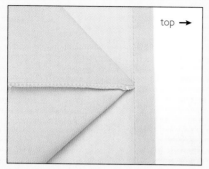

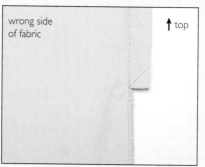

10. Hand stitch along the previous stitchline. Press.

11. On the wrong side and with both edges of the placket together, pin and stitch a diagonal line at the folded base of the placket.

12. Press the right side of the placket under and leave the left side extended.

Field of Flowers, AS&E 57

Boy Blue, AS&E 33

SLEEVE PLACKETS

A sleeve placket can be created using the same methods as a back skirt placket. If a close fitting cuff is required at the bottom of a long sleeve, a placket will be essential to enable the wearer's hand to fit through.

SASHES, BELTS AND CUMMERBUNDS

Sashes and belts help to control fullness while providing a focal point at the back of the garment.

A sash, usually tied into a bow, is a soft and pretty finish while a belt gives a more tailored look to a garment.

The Little Princess, AS&E 37

Driftwood, AS&E 30

Young Love, AS&E 55

Love Hearts, AS&E 58

Taj Mahal, AS&E 26

Sunday Best, AS&E 53

Checkmate, AS&E 27

Star Quality, AS&E 53

MAKING A SASH - DOUBLE LAYER

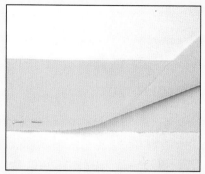

1. Cut two strips of fabric the required width and length.

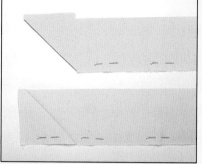

2. With right sides together and matching raw edges, fold each strip in half along the length and pin. Fold one end of each strip as shown and press.

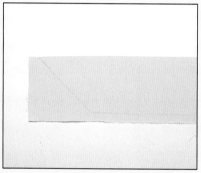

3. Unfold. Stitch down the long raw edge and diagonally across the crease at the end.

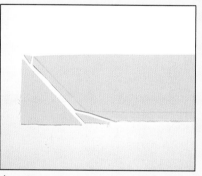

4. Trim the seams and clip the corners.

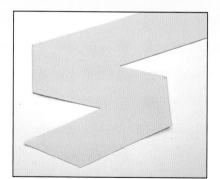

5. Turn to the right side and press.

Fairy Dust, AS&E 51

SASHES

Sashes can be made in various widths from one or two strips of fabric sewn together. For a lighter finish, use a single layer that has been hemmed or finished around all edges. They can also be made with bound edges and firm, wide ribbon may also be used. The most common style of sash has straight edges and a diagonally finished end. Sashes may have shaped edges and ends, and may be trimmed with embroidery or lace.

Embroidery is best worked before the sash is constructed. Avoid any trim that may be damaged when the sash is tied. The sash is inserted into the side seams of a dress with the lower edge level with the back bodice seam and the lower edge of the smocking on the front. Make a left and a right sash.

When the sash is wide, the end is pleated or gathered before it is attached to the garment. Sash keepers hold the sash bow in place, preventing it from hanging down the back of the dress.

Lavender Mist, AS&E 60

ATTACHING THE SASH AT THE EDGE OF THE SMOCKING

On some garments the smocking finishes before the side seam. In this case the sash should be attached at the edge of the smocking, not in the seam.

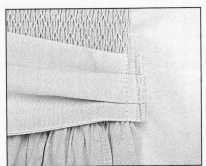

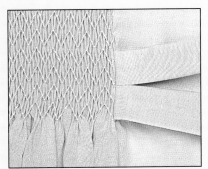

1. Neaten the raw end of the sash. With right sides together and matching the sash stitchline with the edge of the smocking, pin and stitch in place.

2. Fold the sash back on itself, covering the neatened edge. Topstitch if required.

SASH LENGTH CHART

Length to cut sashes so that the sash tip falls 5cm (2") above the finished mid calf hem when tied in a bow.

Age	Sash length	
1 year	70cm	27 1/2 "
18 months	75cm	29 1/2 "
2 years	80cm	31 1/2 "
3 years	85cm	33 1/2 "
4 years	90cm	35 1/2 "
5 years	95cm	37 1/2 "
6 years	100cm	39 1/2 "
7 years	105cm	41 1/2 "
8 years	110cm	43 1/2 "
9 years	115cm	45 1/4 "
10 years	120cm	47 1/4 "

A Red, Red Rose, AS&E 50

HOW TO TIE A SASH

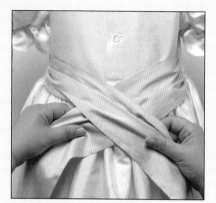

1. Holding a tie in each hand, cross the left tie over the right.

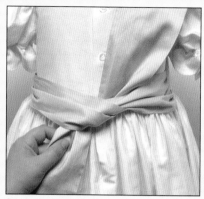

2. Bring the left tie under the right at the centre. Pull the left tie through and leave aside.

3. Make a loop with the right tie.

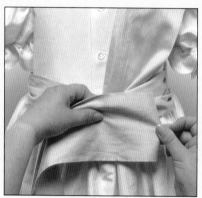

4. Turn the loop to the right.

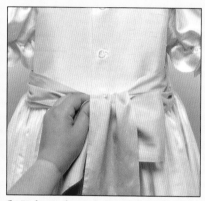

5. Pick up the unlooped tie and place it over the looped tie.

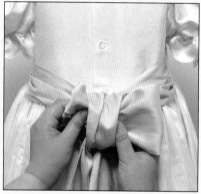

6. Bring the left tie under the looped tie and through the gap underneath.

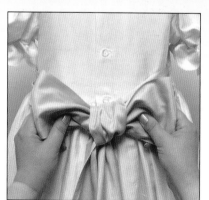

7. Pull on the looped ends to form the bow.

8. Adjust the size of the loops and arrange the ties as required.

Sweet Cinnamon, AS&E 65

MAKING AND ATTACHING A CUMMERBUND

A cummerbund can be attached or unattached and consists of a wide pleated or gathered front band and ties. When using a cummerbund on a smocked garment, it is not necessary to smock under the band but the fullness of the skirt must be controlled to prevent the band from riding up. This can be done by working rows of gathering at the base of the area to be covered or by backsmocking.
The cummerbund will sit nicely if the front lining is a flat panel that has been reinforced with interfacing.

Heaven Sent, AS&E 51

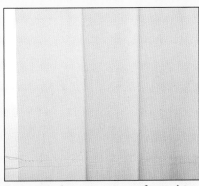

1. Stitch two rows of machine gathering at the position for the lower edge of the bodice on the front panel. Flatten the fabric for pleating.

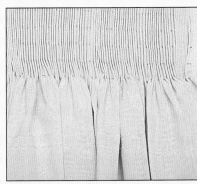

2. Pleat the required number of rows above the gathering.

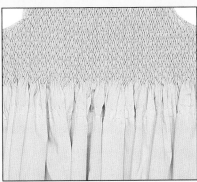

3. Smock the front panel then cut the bodice shaping.

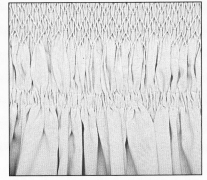

4. Pull up the gathering threads to fit the blocking guide. Distribute the gathers evenly and tie off.

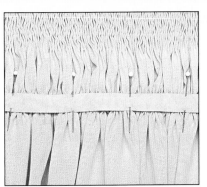

5. On the wrong side of the bodice, pin a length of ribbon or woven tape across the gathering rows.

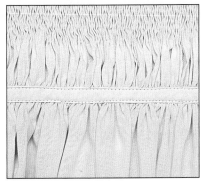

6. From the wrong side, stitch the ribbon or tape in place along both edges. Remove the gathering threads.

MAKING AND ATTACHING A CUMMERBUND... CONTINUED

A cummerbund is an effective way of extending the depth of the bodice without needing to pleat or smock the area that is covered by the band. A cummerbund is usually wider than a sash so it is particularly suited to garments for older children.

Prima Ballerina, AS&E 63

A Red, Red Rose, AS&E 50

Bliss, AS&E 47

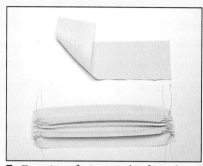

7. Fuse interfacing to the front band lining. Gather or pleat the ends of the band to fit the lining.

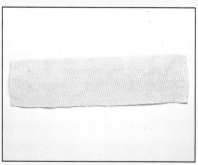

8. With right sides together and matching raw edges, pin and stitch the pieces together along the long edges.

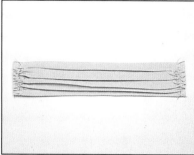

9. Turn to the right side and press the seams. Tack the layers together along the short edges.

10. Pin and tack the front band in place across the front skirt.

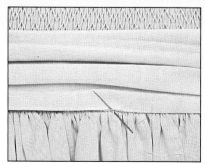

11. If desired, the lower edge of the band can be hand stitched to the front skirt.

12. With right sides together and matching raw edges, position one sash over the cummerbund and tack in place.

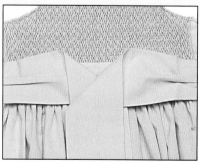

13. Repeat for the second sash. The front is now ready to be attached to the back at the side seams.

FABRIC KEEPERS

Made from the same fabric as the garment, these keepers coordinate perfectly and can be made as long and wide as necessary. They can be decorated with embroidery. The lower end can be caught in the back bodice/skirt seam or stitched on at the same time as the upper end. Make all keepers as a continuous strip. Cut the strip the required length (plus seam allowances) and twice the finished width (plus seam allowances).

Chasing Rainbows, AS&E 28

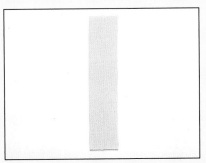

1. With right sides together and matching raw edges, pin and stitch the long edges of the strip together.

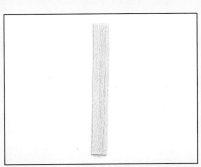

2. Trim the seam and press open. Turn to the right side and press.

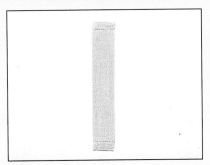

3. Neaten the raw ends.

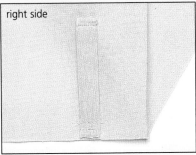

4. Position the keeper on the back bodice. Pin and stitch in place within the seam allowance.

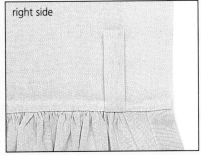

5. After the garment is constructed, fold under the remaining raw end of the keeper.

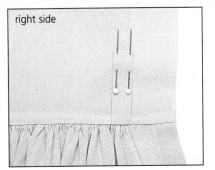

6. Pin in place on the back bodice.

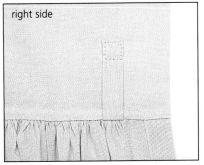

7. Hand or machine stitch in place through both the bodice and lining.

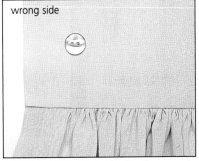

8. If necessary, stitch the keeper in place through a button on the wrong side to prevent the bodice fabric from tearing.

THREAD KEEPERS

A thread keeper is hand stitched after the garment has been completed. Thread keepers are less visible than fabric keepers but are not suitable for very heavy belts or sashes. They can be worked as blanket stitch or chain loops.

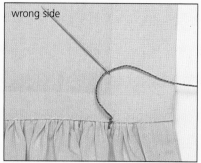

1. Secure the thread on the wrong side through the seam at the lower edge of the back bodice.

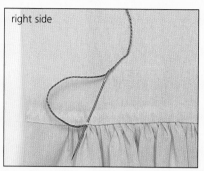

2. Take the thread to the front through the seam. Make a small stitch at the base of the thread.

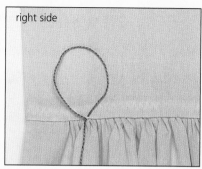

3. Pull the thread through until a loop remains.

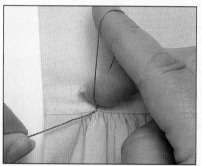

4. Hold the loop open with two fingers of the right hand. Hold the working thread with the left hand.

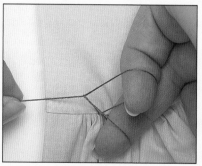

5. Hook the working thread through the loop with the index finger.

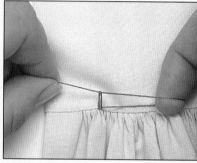

6. Release the first loop and begin to slide it down onto the fabric.

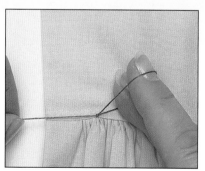

7. Tighten the first loop.

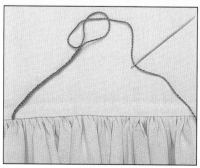

8. Repeat steps 4 - 7 until the desired length is achieved. Take the working thread through the loop.

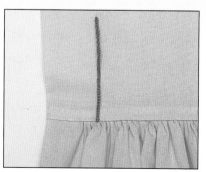

9. Tighten the loop. Take the thread to the back at the position for the top of the keeper and secure.

SLEEVES

There are numerous styles of sleeves that are suited to smocked garments. Sleeves that are gathered around the sleeve head are most commonly used as this fullness balances the generous skirt on a smocked garment. Sleeves that are overly full can make a garment look top heavy and unbalanced. A petticoat under the dress can rectify this problem. Smocking can be used to control the fullness at the lower edge of short or long sleeves, as can a band or binding. Sleeves that are finished with smocking are cut with a straight lower edge. Sleeves that are gathered into a band are cut with a curved lower edge.

The Bluebird, AS&E 49

Jacaranda Blue, AS&E 39

The Godchild, AS&E 53

Gathering Rosebuds, AS&E 29

The Divine Dropwaist, AS&E 37

Carousel, AS&E 63

Celia, AS&E 56

PIPING THE UPPER EDGE OF THE SLEEVE BAND

Piping helps to stabilise the seam when a gathered sleeve is joined to a flat band.
When piping only the upper edge of the band, the band and lining can be cut as a single piece.

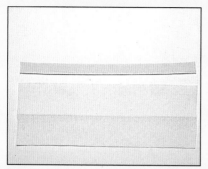

1. Cut a length of piping to fit the sleeve band. Remove the piping cord from the seam allowance.

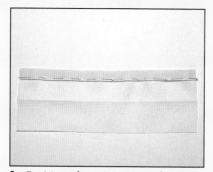

2. Position the piping on the right side of the upper edge of the band. The piping stitchline is aligned with the band stitchline. Pin in place.

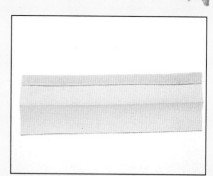

3. Stitch along the piping stitchline.

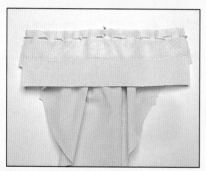

4. Mark the centre of the sleeve edge and the band with a pin. Pull up the gathering threads on the sleeve to fit the band. With right sides together, pin the piped band to the lower sleeve.

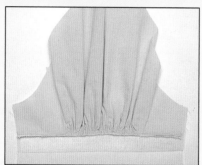

5. Stitch in place between the corded edge of the piping and the previous stitchline. Remove the gathering threads. Trim and neaten the seam. Press towards the band.

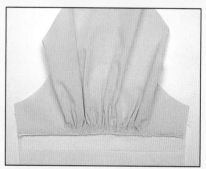

6. Press under the seam allowance on the remaining long edge of the band lining. The band is finished after the underarm seam is stitched.

SLEEVE BAND AND BINDING CUTTING CHART	Size	Newborn	3m	6m	12m	18m	2yr	3yr
	Sleeve bands 7cm (2¾") wide	20cm (8")	21cm (8¼")	21.5cm (8½")	21.5cm (8½")	22cm (8⅝")	22.5cm (8⅞")	23cm (9")
	Binding 5.5cm (2¼") wide							
	Size	**4yr**	**5yr**	**6yr**	**7yr**	**8yr**	**9yr**	**10yr**
	Sleeve bands 9cm (3½") wide	23.5cm (9¼")	24.5cm (9⅝")	25cm (9¾")	26cm (10¼")	26.5cm (10½")	27cm (10⅝")	27.5cm (10¾")
	Binding 5.5cm (2¼") wide							

PIPING THE UPPER AND LOWER EDGES OF THE SLEEVE BAND

Cut two pieces of piping the same length as the band for each sleeve.

Country Garland, AS&E 44

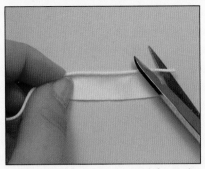

1. Remove the piping cord from the seam allowance.

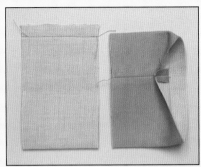

2. With right sides together, pin and stitch the underarm seam of each band and lining. Trim the seams and press open. Turn to the right side.

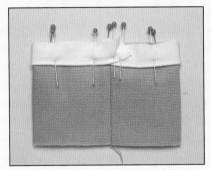

3. Beginning at the seam and leaving a 1cm (⅜") tail, pin the piping to the right side of the band. Overlap the ends and curve tails as shown. Baste.

4. Repeat for the lower edge of the band. Stitch along the piping stitchline on both edges.

5. With right sides together and matching seams and edges, pin the lining to lower edge of band. Stitch just inside the previous stitchline. Trim the seam.

6. With right sides together and matching raw edges and seams, pin the upper edge of the band to the sleeve. Adjust the sleeve gathers to fit. Keep the lining free.

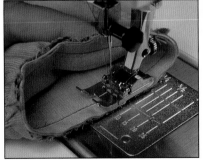

7. Stitch between the corded edge of the piping and the previous stitchline.

8. Trim the seam, press towards the band. Press under 1cm (⅜") on the raw edge of the lining. Trim to 5mm (³⁄₁₆").

PIPING THE UPPER AND LOWER EDGES OF THE SLEEVE BAND... CONTINUED

9. Fold the lining to the inside. Pin with the fold aligned with the previous stitchline. Hand stitch in place.

10. Turn to the right side and press.

Rose Red, AS&E 28

FINISHING THE SLEEVE EDGE WITH A PIPED BINDING

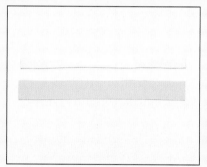

1. Fold the bias strip in half along its length and press. Cut a length of piping to fit. Remove the piping cord from the seam allowance.

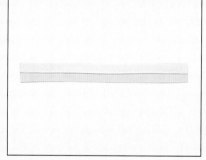

2. Matching raw edges and stitchlines, pin and stitch the piping to the binding.

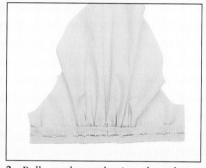

3. Pull up the gathering threads on the sleeve to fit the binding. With right sides together and aligning stitchlines, pin the piped edge to the lower sleeve.

4. Stitch in place. Trim the seam.

5. After stitching the underarm seam, fold the binding to the wrong side, enclosing the seam. Hand stitch in place.

6. Completed sleeve.

SLEEVE PUFFS

To maintain the puff of the sleeve, a bias fold of stiff fabric such as organdy, organza or tulle can be stitched in with the sleeve. This will hold the sleeve head nicely. Binding the armhole seam will prevent the cut edges of the stiff fabric scratching. Cut a square of fabric large enough to fit the sleeve head once the square is folded in half diagonally.

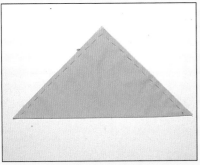

1. Fold the square in half to form a triangle. Tack the layers together as indicated. Do not press the folded edge.

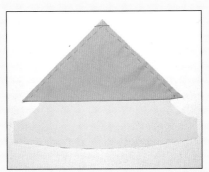

2. Position the triangle over the wrong side of the sleeve.

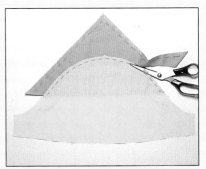

3. Tack the layers together. Trim away the excess.

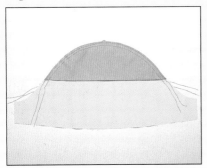

4. Work two rows of machine gathering around the sleeve head between the marks indicated on the pattern.

5. Insert the sleeve using your chosen method.

Devotion, AS&E 53

SLEEVE INTERLINING

Sleeves made from very soft, sheer fabrics such as georgette and chiffon can be lined with organdy, organza or tulle. This will retain the sheerness but hold the head of the sleeve up, maintaining the puff. Cut two sleeves from both the fabric and lining. Tack the two layers together around the entire outer edge of each sleeve. Treat as one piece.

STITCHING THE UNDERARM SEAM - SMOCKED LOWER EDGE

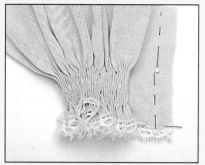

1. With right sides together and matching raw and lower edges, pin the sleeve together along the underarm seam.

2. Stitch. Trim and neaten the seam.

3. Press the seam towards the back.

STITCHING THE UNDERARM SEAM - WITH SLEEVE BAND

Before pinning the underarm seam, open out the folded edge on the sleeve band lining.

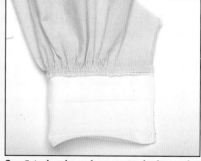

1. With right sides together and matching raw edges, piping and folded edge, pin the sleeve together along the underarm seam.

2. Stitch the sleeve, including the band and lining. Trim and neaten the seam.

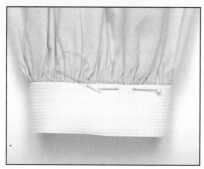

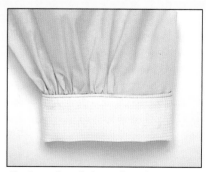

3. Press the seam towards the back. Refold the lower edge of the sleeve band lining.

4. Fold the band lining to the wrong side. Hand stitch in place along the previous stitchline. Press.

5. Completed sleeve band.

INSERTING THE SLEEVES - METHODS 1 AND 2

In method 1 the underarm seam is stitched after the sleeve is attached to the garment.
Method 2 is also known as setting in the sleeve and the underarm seam is stitched prior to inserting it.

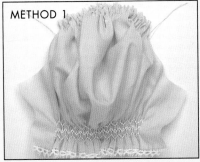

1. Pull up the gathers to fit the armhole.

2. With right sides together and matching raw edges, marks, shoulder seam and sleeve centre, pin the sleeve into the armhole.

3. Stitch. Trim and neaten the seam. Remove the gathering threads. Carefully press the seam toward the sleeve.

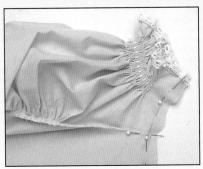

4. With right sides together and matching raw edges, armhole seams and lower sleeve edges, pin the sleeve underarm seam and side seam.

5. Stitch, trim and neaten the seam. Press the seam towards the back.

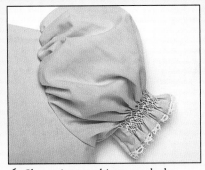

6. Sleeve inserted into armhole.

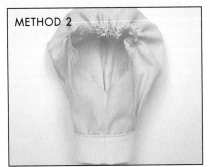

1. Pull up the gathers to fit the armhole.

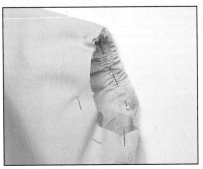

2. With right sides together and matching raw edges, marks, shoulder seam and sleeve centre, pin the sleeve into the corresponding armhole.

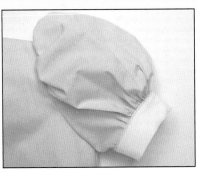

3. Stitch. Remove the gathering threads. Trim and neaten the seam. Carefully press the seam toward the sleeve.

INSERTING THE SLEEVES - METHOD 3

This method combines the previous two methods.

1. Pull up the gathers to fit the armhole.

2. With right sides together and matching raw edges, marks, shoulder seam and sleeve centre, pin the sleeve into the armhole.

3. Stitch, beginning and ending 2.5cm (1") from the underarm. Remove the gathering threads.

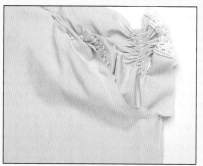

4. With right sides together and matching raw edges, stitch the side seam. Trim and neaten. Press towards the back.

5. With right sides together and matching raw and lower sleeve edges, pin the sleeve together at the underarm. Stitch. Trim and neaten the seam. Press.

HINT

When using silk fabric, neaten the tops of the sleeves before assembling them. Silk frays on the top of the sleeve curve.

Cassie, AS&E 54

6. With right sides together and matching raw edges and seams, stitch the remaining part of the sleeve to the armhole. Trim and neaten the armhole seam.

7. Sleeve inserted into armhole.

TAILORED SLEEVES - EASING IN A SLEEVE HEAD

Before inserting the sleeve, the excess fullness above the seamline must be controlled. This is done by stitching easing rows either side of the stitchline. These are removed once the sleeve has been inserted.

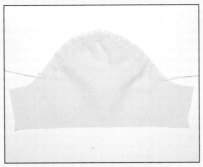

1. Adjust the straight stitch to the maximum length. Beginning at the marked point at one side of the sleeve, work a row of machine stitching 5mm (³⁄₁₆") from the raw edge. Work a second row 15mm (⁵⁄₈") from the raw edge.

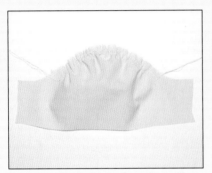

2. Using the bobbin threads, pull up both rows slightly.

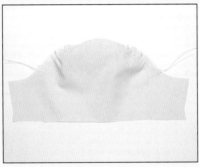

3. Flatten the fabric only between the easing rows as much as possible. Using a steam iron press the fabric between the two easing rows to ease out any gathers.

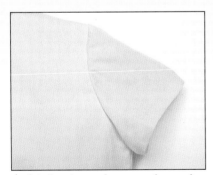

4. Stitch, trim and neaten the underarm seam. With right sides together and matching raw edges and marks, pin the sleeve into the corresponding armhole. Stitch, adjusting where necessary. Remove the easing threads. Trim and neaten the seam.

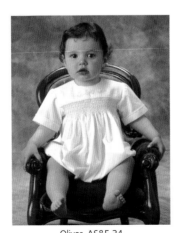

Oliver, AS&E 34

HINT

When pressing sleeves, carefully press the seam towards the sleeve, taking care not to press the gathers.

When the seam is pressed towards the sleeve, a puffed sleeve 'stands up'. When the seam is pressed towards the bodice, a puffed sleeve is flat.

The seam pressed towards the bodice

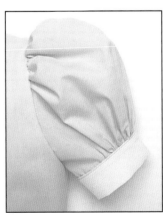

The seam pressed towards the sleeve

ANGEL SLEEVES

An angel sleeve is not a sleeve at all but a strip of fabric gathered or smocked to form a frill that sits over the top of the arm. It can be a single thickness hemmed on the outer edge, or a double thickness of fabric cut on the straight grain or bias. When using an angel sleeve in a bishop garment, the lower edge of the armhole is usually finished with a binding.

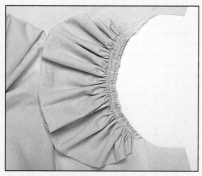

1. Pull up the gathers on the frill to fit. With right sides together, matching raw edges and the centre of the frill to the shoulder seam, pin the frill to the marked position on the armhole. Stitch.

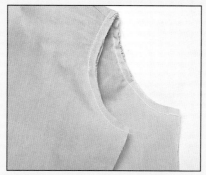

2. With right sides together and matching shoulder seams, fold the bodice lining over the bodice, sandwiching the frill between. Pin and stitch around the entire armhole. Remove the gathering threads.

3. Trim the seam and clip the curves. Turn the bodice to the right side by bringing the back bodice through the tunnel formed at the shoulders. Press.

4. Understitch the front armhole by stitching from the underarm to the shoulder seam through the lining and the seam allowance beneath. Repeat for the back armhole.

HINTS

Smock the lower edge of long sleeves. When the child's arms grow, unpick the smocking and the hemmed edge and gather the sleeve onto a band.

If a sleeve is to be embellished with embroidery, tucks, lace insertion or any other form of decoration, complete this before the sleeve is cut out.

If you are working with fabric that stretches, such as a knit fabric, stitch with the bodice uppermost. For a tailored sleeve, ease in any fullness by stretching the armhole to fit the sleeve head.

Spirit of Adventure, AS&E 34

YOUR FINISHED GARMENT

PRESSING

Once the garment is complete, remove all traces of fabric marker lines with a water spray or damp cloth. Press the garment, taking care not to press the smocking. For the final press on collars, try finger pressing to avoid pressing in ridges or making impressions.

Fill puffed sleeves with tissue paper to prevent them from becoming crushed. Leave the sashes untied. Place the garment onto a padded hanger and hang in a well aired position.

If the garment is to be stored for any length of time, ensure that it is protected from moths and other nasty insects.

WASHING

Note the care requirements when purchasing fabric and threads. If you are unsure of the colour fastness of the threads you choose, test wash a sample to check for colour bleeding. Stitch some thread onto a scrap of your chosen fabric and treat as you would the finished garment.

Smocked garments that can be laundered should be hand washed to protect the smocking from being overly agitated in a washing machine. If you choose to machine wash, select a gentle cycle. Dry away from direct sunlight to protect from fading.

STORAGE

Heirloom garments often need to be stored for many years. Ensure that the garment is spotlessly clean before storing. Carefully fold the garment, placing layers of acid free tissue between the folds. Place in an acid free cardboard box with an insect repellant. Do not store natural fibres in plastic as the fibres will sweat and this can cause mildew.

HINT

To prevent small puffed sleeves from becoming wrinkled, fill the sleeves with plastic bags after washing. The fabric will dry without creases and need very little ironing.

Blossom, AS&E 65